TWAYNE'S WORLD AUTHORS SERIES

A Survey of the World's Literature

Sylvia E. Bowman, Indiana University

GENERAL EDITOR

GERMANY

Ulrich Weisstein, Indiana University

EDITOR

Heinrich Mann

(TWAS 27)

TWAYNE'S WORLD AUTHORS SERIES (TWAS)

*The purpose of TWAS is to survey the major writers
—novelists, dramatists, historians, poets, philosophers,
and critics—of the nations of the world. Among the
national literatures covered are those of Australia,
Canada, China, Eastern Europe, France, Germany,
Greece, India, Italy, Japan, Latin America, New Zea-
land, Poland, Russia, Scandinavia, Spain, and the
African nations, as well as Hebrew, Yiddish, and
Latin Classical literatures. This survey is comple-
mented by Twayne's United States Authors Series
and English Authors Series*

*The intent of each volume in these series is to present
a critical-analytical study of the works of the writer;
to include biographical and historical material that
may be necessary for understanding, appreciation,
and critical appraisal of the writer; and to present all
material in clear, concise English—but not to vitiate
the scholarly content of the work by doing so.*

Heinrich Mann

By ROLF N. LINN

University of California, Santa Barbara

Twayne Publishers, Inc. :: New York

To the memory of my father

Preface

HEINRICH MANN is well known in some European countries, less known in others, and virtually unknown in the Anglo-Saxon world. Apart from dissertations, the present study is the first book in English about him and his work. It is therefore conceived as a critical introduction. A brief account of his life, designated as the first chapter, is followed by an appraisal of his major literary achievements in chronological order. Some stories and essays are mentioned in conjunction with other writings only, and a large portion of his enormous output is not mentioned at all. These exclusions were deemed necessary in the interest of a coherent presentation.

Chapter II deals with the two novels which Heinrich Mann himself regarded as the beginnings of his literary career. The third chapter encompasses all the novels and the most important novellas of his first period. His turn from estheticism to social criticism, manifest in the writings published between 1910 and 1918, is discussed in chapter IV, the following chapter being concerned with Mann's literary activities during the years of the Weimar Republic. The sixth chapter is devoted to a reading of the two-volume novel about Henry IV of France, the only significant contribution to letters made by the author during his eight years in French exile. His American decade, the last of his life, yielded three novels, one fragment and one autobiographical work, which are scrutinized in chapter VII.

In view of the fact that only a small portion of Mann's writings has been translated into English, and that some British and American editions were published under different titles, German titles are used throughout the text. The selected bibliography at the end lists the translations with their English titles. The notes and references enable the reader to gain an impression of the state of Heinrich Mann criticism. They also constitute an acknowledgment of the debt which I owe to my predecessors.

Numerous specialized Heinrich Mann studies whose authors quite naturally emphasize a particular aspect at the expense of all others have appeared over the years. One can study a single work in great detail; one can dwell at length on Mann's formative years before 1900. One can ferret out influences and show the origin of many an idea, a phrase, or a sentence. But in so doing one cannot help losing sight of the total personality and the total accomplishment of the man whom one has chosen as a subject exactly because he was found generally intriguing and deserving of attention in the first place. This does not diminish the value of specialized investigations at all, but it accounts for the eclectic use of earlier scholarship which I found mandatory if I was to avoid gross distortion in my survey.

Although every thorough intellectual history of twentieth century Germany must consider the less famous of the brothers Mann, his place in literature is neither fixed nor as yet assured. This is as much the fault of his uncritical admirers as it is that of his detractors. It must be admitted, however, that the author himself did much to mislead both groups. He often directed their attention to his ideas, his moral position, and his political concerns. Consequently they underrated or ignored—at least until recent years—his awareness of the human condition and his ability to put his insights into excellent prose. Furthermore, his work is uneven. At its worst it sinks to the level of the penny novel; at its best it is a singularly powerful expression of man's struggle for harmony within and without. I have endeavored to stress the best, since an author has the right to be judged by it. Where for certain reasons less than first-rate works are discussed, I have given my opinion candidly. Lately a number of critics have begun to cope with the problems of differentiation and selection which Heinrich Mann's *oeuvre* calls for. Wholesome disagreements have developed. It appears to be a legitimate secondary aim of the following pages to join in their debate.

ROLF N. LINN

University of California

Acknowledgments

I wish to express my gratitude to the following organizations and individuals:

To the University of California at Santa Barbara for a research grant in connection with this book.

To the Heinrich Mann Archives in East Berlin for permission to inspect unpublished material and for the use of photographs of Heinrich Mann.

To the Schiller National Museum in Marbach, Germany, for making available numerous Heinrich Mann letters.

To Oswald Wolff Publishers, London, for permission to quote from W. E. Yuill, "Heinrich Mann," *German Men of Letters*, II (1963).

To the University of Wisconsin Press for permission to make use of my article, "Heinrich Mann's 'Die Branzilla,'" *Monatshefte*, 1958.

To *Modern Language Quarterly* for permission to make use of my article, "Heinrich Mann and the German Inflation," *MLQ*, 1962.

To Professors Edmond Masson and Harry Steinhauer for their interest in the book and their many constructive suggestions.

To Professor Ulrich Weisstein, to whom I am doubly indebted. His basic historical and bibliographical work on Heinrich Mann proved invaluable, and his editorial acumen accounts for numerous improvements of the text.

Contents

Contents

Chronology

1871 Birth of Luiz Heinrich Mann in Lübeck, as the oldest son of the grain merchant Johann Thomas Heinrich Mann and Julia née da Silva-Bruhns.

1889 Finishes Gymnasium.

1890 Goes to Dresden to learn the book trade.

1891 Moves to Berlin. Works for S. Fischer Publishers, and studies at Berlin University.

1893 After his father's death the family moves to Munich. Heinrich's first trip to Paris.

1893- Extensive travels in Italy.
1898

1894 Publication of Mann's first novel, *In einer Familie.*

1899- Sojourn in Munich, Berlin, Italy, France.
1914

1900 *Im Schlaraffenland.*

1903 *Die Göttinnen; Die Jagd nach Liebe.*

1905 *Flöten und Dolche* (containing "Pippo Spano"); *Professor Unrat.*

1907 *Zwischen den Rassen.*

1908 *Die Bösen* ("Die Branzilla" and "Der Tyrann").

1909 *Die kleine Stadt.*

1911 *Die Rückkehr vom Hades* (contains "Auferstehung").

1913 *Madame Legros.*

1914 Marriage to Maria Kanova.

1914- Domicile Munich.
1927

1915 "Zola" (In *Die weissen Blätter*).

1917 *Die Armen.*

1918 *Der Untertan.*

1919 *Macht und Mensch.*

1924   *Abrechnungen* (contains "Der Gläubiger" and "Sterny").

1925   *Der Kopf,* "Kobes."

1926   Member of the Prussian Academy of the Arts.

1927   *Mutter Marie.*

1928   *Eugenie oder Die Bürgerzeit.*

1929   Moves to Berlin. *Sieben Jahre: Chronik der Gedanken und Vorgänge.*

1930   *Die grosse Sache.*

1931   *Geist und Tat: Franzosen 1780–1930.* President of the literary section of the Prussian Academy of the Arts.

1932   *Ein ernstes Leben.*

1933   *Das Bekenntnis zum Übernationalen.* Emigration to France with second wife Nelly Kroeger. Revocation of German citizenship.

1933-   Domicile in Nice. Frequent trips to Paris in behalf of re-
1940   sistance movement. Collaboration with *Volksfront.*

1935   *Die Jugend des Königs Henri Quatre.*

1938   *Die Vollendung des Königs Henri Quatre.*

1940   Flight to the United States.

1940-   Domicile in Beverly Hills and Los Angeles.
1950

1943   *Lidice.*

1944   Death of Nelly Mann.

1945   *Ein Zeitalter wird besichtigt.*

1947   Honorary doctorate, Humboldt University, East Berlin.

1949   *Der Atem.*

1950   Death in Los Angeles.

1956   *Empfang bei der Welt.*

1958   *Die traurige Geschichte von Friedrich dem Grossen* (fragment).

1961   Transfer of ashes to Berlin.

CHAPTER 1

Heinrich Mann's Life

LUIZ HEINRICH MANN was born in 1871, the same year that saw the birth of the German Empire, whose keenest critic he was to become. His father, Johann Thomas Heinrich Mann, was a prosperous grain merchant and ship-owner in the old Hanseatic town of Lübeck, who could trace his family back to the middle of the seventeenth century. Since 1790 the Manns had been citizens of the free city on the Baltic. His mother Julia née da Silva-Bruhns was a descendant, on her maternal side, from Portuguese settlers in Brazil, while her father was also a native of Lübeck. Both the patrician background and the Portuguese ancestry were to play a considerable role in the works of her first-born.

Heinrich was the oldest of five children. His brother Thomas was four years younger than he. His sisters Julia and Carla followed, the latter, ten years his junior, being his favorite sibling; and in 1890 Viktor was born, who shortly before his death published a book about the Mann family.[1]

Senator Mann—the father became a senator of the city state in 1877—hoped that Heinrich would follow in his footsteps, but the latter showed no interest in either the grain and shipping business or in city government.[2] Not believing that his oldest son was gifted enough to be more than a literary dilettante, the Senator, in a draft of his will, urged the guardians of his children to oppose Heinrich's inclinations toward "a so-called literary career," and charged his brother to exercise his influence on Heinrich so that the latter "might not end up on the wrong path leading to misfortune."[3] But in 1948 Heinrich wrote, "To the twenty-year-old the dying man said, 'I want to help you,' to become a writer: it was clear to both of them; the one kissed the hand of the other; he still kisses it today."[4]

In 1889 Heinrich left the Gymnasium. His restless mind did

not let him stay long in any one place. First he went to Dresden to learn the book trade. The year 1890 found him in Berlin working for the publishing house of Samuel Fischer. In 1891 his father died, leaving a sufficient estate to allow him to pursue his literary interests. The major portion of the next decade Heinrich spent in Italy, especially in Florence and Rome; but Germany, Switzerland, and Austria also saw him as a guest, in part because of his precarious health. When writing to Karl Lemke in 1947, he recalled sojourns in Berlin, Wiesbaden, Lausanne, Paris, Munich, Ultental, South Tyrol, Walchensee; and he despaired of recalling them all.[5]

The years before the turn of the century Heinrich Mann later dismissed as rather insignificant. He called them "a decade which was without duties, without a work." [6] At the same time he understood them to be a formative period in his life. They were indeed. Not only did he learn to know the Italian people and the German political situation; not only did he become acquainted with the works of Nietzsche, D'Annunzio, and the major nineteenth century French authors; he also improved his craftsmanship. By the time his first successful novel appeared in 1900, he had published one immature novel, one translation, six book reviews, and two collections of short stories. In addition, he had edited a journal, contributing thirty-one signed articles to it, another score being most likely also from his pen.[7]

Beginning with the year 1900, Mann entered upon a period of extraordinary productivity. In that year he published his novel *Im Schlaraffenland* (*In the Land of Cockaigne*). The year 1903 saw the completion of both *Die Göttinnen* ("The Goddesses") and *Die Jagd nach Liebe* ("Pursuit of Love"). Three further novels appeared in the odd years of the first decade of the new century; *Professor Unrat* (*The Blue Angel*) in 1905, *Zwischen den Rassen* ("Between the Races") in 1907, and *Die kleine Stadt* (*The Little Town*) in 1909. Simultaneously he published nineteen novellas and short stories as well as a number of translations and essays.

Having already mentioned Mann's financial independence, his restlessness, and his health problems, one needs to add only a few facts of significance regarding his private life in what was to become known as his "first period." One such fact was his closeness to his brother Thomas. Thomas joined Heinrich in Italy in 1895, where the two, intermittently, spent approximately three years together. Though not as entwined in their collaboration as the Brothers Goncourt the two Manns shared many experiences and exchanged many ideas. When Thomas, in a conversation with this writer in 1947, recalled how they invented the name "Buddenbrook" together, he spoke with great warmth of that far-away period of vigor and hope. Other friendships of lasting effect were those with Frank Wedekind and Arthur Schnitzler. A major event in Heinrich's life during this time was the death of his sister Carla in 1910. Carla's suicide "did not paralyze his creativity," but "the sad occurrence was forever engraved in his memory." [8] And finally one must mention Heinrich's marriage, later dissolved, to the actress Maria Kanova in August of 1914. But when it took place, Heinrich had already entered his second phase, and World War I had broken out.

The war saw the brothers Mann ideologically in different camps. Thomas sided with the Germans, defending the German soul. In a letter to Stefan Zweig he called his attitude an "exceedingly modest chauvinism." [9] Heinrich, on the other hand, had always been suspicious of German "profundity," which avoided coping with the problems of political freedom. Therefore, he wished for a German defeat. And so in 1915 he attacked Thomas publicly, with Thomas reciprocating in 1918. As a consequence, the two brothers ceased to be friends for several years. But both longed for a reconciliation, which came about when Heinrich underwent major surgery. Accompanying the flowers sent by Thomas to Heinrich's bedside in January, 1922, was a note saying, "Dear Heinrich, take these flowers and cordial greetings and good wishes;—I could not send them sooner. The days behind us were difficult, but now we are over the worst and will walk better,—together, if your heart feels like mine." [10] Once the friendship was restored, it endured for life.

The second phase of Heinrich's life as a writer, encompassing the period from 1910 to the advent of Hitler, is marked by the rejection of his earlier estheticism, and by the assumption of the role of social critic. Two essays of the year 1910 revealed his new program. Then followed *Der Untertan* (*The Patrioteer*) as the first of three novels about the empire of William II, the famous Zola essay, and a play about Madame Legros. The second part of the trilogy was also completed by 1917, but, for the rest, the war years yielded only ephemeral essays from the author's pen. Gradually his reputation grew. His earlier works, not very popular until 1916, suddenly found a broad market. In 1943 Mann recalled wistfully, "Georg Heinrich Meyer, Director of the Kurt Wolff Publishing House, recognized the moment in 1916. Suddenly he sold of the six novels of my 'first period' three-quarters of a million copies. Up to then, they had had, all in all, sales of a few thousand." [11] Such public acclaim brought with it numerous obligations that were destined adversely to affect Mann's literary output during the years of the Weimar Republic.

Ulrich Weisstein, in the most scholarly book on Heinrich Mann yet written, states correctly that the author served in the early years of the Republic as warner and mentor, while being only indirectly active politically from 1920 to 1925.[12] Yet Mann's public speeches and innumerable journalistic efforts for the young democracy led Hofmannsthal to wonder whether the one-time master of German prose was going to devote himself completely to a career in politics.[13] But Mann's multifarious activities in behalf of the preservation of the Weimar Republic on the one hand and German-French understanding on the other—undertaken with a healthy pessimism—did not consume all of his energies. Up to the time of Hitler's rise to power, he managed to complete five novels and a large number of novellas, some of the latter belonging among his best writings.

Outwardly, 1931 marks the high point in Mann's career. He was elected President of the Literary Section of the Prussian Academy of the Arts. He was as famous in France as he was in Germany. Undisputed leader in the field of *Kulturpolitik,* he went on one lecture tour after another, and on the occasion of his sixtieth birthday he was honored and celebrated in such a way that one writer stated, "Heinrich Mann's creativity is so much an article of faith today that doubts concerning the appropriateness of this faith are no longer allowed, even after the birthday celebration is over." [14] When, in the following year, the question of a successor to President Hindenburg arose, the journalist Kurt Hiller could seriously propose Mann as a candidate.

This proposal, like many honors bestowed upon him, contained one of the great misunderstandings concerning Mann's activities.

He was not a party politician; he was not even a member of a party. His ideal was the creation of a European atmosphere in which the best in man would have an opportunity to unfold. In his last essay written before he was forced to leave Germany, he spoke in favor of a united Europe, giving the following reason: "A single country is no longer viable in Europe, neither economically nor politically, and certainly not morally. Several supra-nationally joined countries have a chance to make their people better and happier." [15] And he saw proof for the rightness of his view in the fact that the greatest achievements of the German mind, like the writings of Goethe and Schiller, had come about before Germany was a nation. The reference to the German classics made it quite clear that cultural growth was his ultimate concern. For its sake alone he indulged in political journalism.

With the nomination of Hitler as Chancellor, Mann's days in Germany were numbered. On February 21, 1933, he left for France, where he was to remain until 1940. During this time he wrote editorials for the *Dépêche de Toulouse,* participated in the *Front Populaire,* and worked on a masterly historical novel about Henry IV. Hitler's occupation of France forced him to flee to the United States. He spent his remaining years there, not too far from the domicile of his brother, writing three more novels and a rather unique volume of memoirs. A novel in dialogue about Frederick the Great was not completed.

In a report about his brother, requested in 1946 by the editors of *Freies Deutschland,* Thomas Mann describes Heinrich's life in California at some length.[16] He gives details about his brother's living quarters, mentions the grievous loss which the death of his second wife had meant to Heinrich, and says this about the latter's mode of existence:

At certain hours of the day he reads German, French and English, aloud whenever the prose is worth it. In the morning, when he had his strong coffee, from seven o'clock until perhaps noon, he writes; produces imperturbably in his boldness and self-assuredness, carried by that faith in the mission of literature that he so often confessed to in words of proud beauty; advances the work at hand by covering sheet after sheet with his exceedingly clear and distinctly developed Roman script, still using a steel pen dipped in ink,—certainly not without effort, for the good is difficult, but with the trained facility of the great worker.[17]

Thomas then lists and appraises the individual works of his older brother. He particularly praises the book of memoirs *Ein Zeitalter wird besichtigt* ("Review of an Age") and ends with the prophecy, "The objective fact that this seventy-five year old man was one of their [the Germans'] most original creative writers will prove stronger than their capriciousness and will sooner or later enter their reluctant conscience." When Heinrich died in 1950, shortly before his eightieth birthday, his brother's prediction had not yet come true, but there are indications in recent years that his faith will be rewarded.

CHAPTER 2

The Twin Foundations

I Cockaigne

"IN 1897 in Rome, 34 Via Argentina, talent overcame me," Heinrich Mann wrote in 1947. "I did not know what I was doing. I thought I was making a penciled draft, but wrote the nearly finished novel. My talent was born in Rome after three years under that city's influence." [1] With this statement, addressed to a potential biographer, Mann indicated that he wanted his earlier efforts to be disregarded. And he was right, for, whatever their merits, it was not until 1900 that he began to prepare the ground for all the works of his first truly creative period, which ended in 1910.

The two novels which form the foundation of Mann's art are as different from one another as can be. The first, *Im Schlaraffenland*, is a social satire; the second, *Die Göttinnen*, constitutes a glorification of estheticism. The former is realistic; the latter gives all too free rein to the imagination. Correspondingly, whereas *Im Schlaraffenland* borrows liberally from the French naturalist school, the trilogy of *Die Göttinnen* often resembles the writings of Huysmans, D'Annunzio, and Oscar Wilde.

Im Schlaraffenland is a social novel depicting the "coarse social strata of bourgeois Berlin." [2] Its main characters are types that gained prominence only after the Franco-Prussian War. Theodor Fontane was the first to introduce them into German literature, in such figures as Ezechiel Van der Straaten and Frau Jenny Treibel. Fontane dealt with them in a good-natured way, since he saw them appear on the scene, but not yet dominate it. In Thomas Mann's *Buddenbrooks* they exist peripherally and as a structural balance in the Hagenström family. They are the upstarts who substitute ambition and strong elbows for good taste and social responsibility. They seek to fill the void left by the decline of a principled upper-middle-class. In Heinrich Mann's novel they are

[21]

recognized as having achieved their aim. They are the new leaders of society.

Without adequate models in the German literary tradition, Heinrich Mann turned to French examples, most importantly to Maupassant's *Bel Ami*. In both novels a young man from the provinces, exercising great fascination over women, finds his way into a life of ease through an affair with the aging wife of a Jewish business tycoon. Getting tired of her, he returns to other women. His mistress' discovery of his unfaithfulness brings about the last major change in his life. Fortunately for him, he knows too much about the machinations of the Jew to be treated according to the latter's true wishes. But where Maupassant's hero succeeds in rising to the highest heights by marrying one of the tycoon's daughters, Mann's protagonist must be satisfied with a modest newspaper job.

There are other parallels as well. Mann's Consul-General Türkheimer makes millions through a fraudulent stock market coup with the shares of a certain Texas company. Maupassant's M. Walter does the same with the stock certificates of some Algerian mines. Both financiers recognized the need for controlling public opinion and combine banking and newspaper enterprises. Bel Ami, whose real name is Georges Duroy, ennobles himself by the simple expedient of changing the spelling of his name to Du Roy. Andreas Zumsee in *Schlaraffenland* also splits his surname to give it distinction, calling himself Zum See. And finally, Bel Ami's young mistress discovers the hair of Mme Walter wound around his coat buttons, while Mrs. Türkheimer finds the plumed hat and a glove near Andreas' desk, thus learning the reason for her lover's coldness and the meaning of the muffled noise in the next room.

In spite of these similarities, Mann's work differs considerably in spirit from *Bel Ami*. Maupassant, though free from the tone of moral indignation often found in the American "muck-raking" novels of the turn of the century, is serious throughout. Mann, on the other hand, treats his subject with humor, even levity, and takes an obvious delight in gentle quips, tongue-in-cheek explanations and clever sarcasms. " 'Tell me,' " someone asks at a party, " 'is it true that Lizzi has jewels on her garters?' " " 'Why not?' " another replies. " 'You can think of several more places where Lizzi may wear jewelry and you'll always be right.' " [3] After the performance of a revolutionary play, Mrs. Türkheimer, learning the name of its author, "shook her head incredulously. 'But he has never written anything. Why should he suddenly spoil his reputation by a play like this?'" (133)

Throughout the novel, criticism takes the form of mockery. "'Nowadays,'" says one Duschnitzki, "'one can make fun of anything, step on anything . . .'" (47); anything, that is, the honor of the middle class, the army, the crowned heads, the reputation of women, and even—this is added with the low voice of awe—of the stock market. Heinrich Mann satirizes all of them.

About the press one character has this to say: "Above all others, the *Evening Courier* has recognized that a partisan press is out of the running. Of course, we stand for a sound liberal economic policy. We'd be crazy if we didn't. . . . Apart from this, we consider ourselves an organ of German spiritual culture." (31) About Türkheimer: "What a great man! I have said it a thousand times: for us moderns, for us literati, there is nothing higher than a genius of action. Napoleon, Bismarck, Türkheimer!" (89) And about the decadent bourgeois and the nobility: "Although he knew nothing about the background of his grandfather, the scion of the vigorous bourgeoisie came at least as close to attaining the ideal of complete idiocy as did Baron von Hochstetten, whose forefathers had entered Brandenburg together with the Count of Nuremberg." (102)

Literature fares no better in the novel than does society. "With visible pleasure," says Ulrich Weisstein, "he parodies the art of decadence, whose gods (Heine, Poe, Baudelaire, Verlaine) are revered by Zum See . . . and the *Fleurs du Mal* addiction of impotent Mrs. Claire Pimbusch. Elsewhere he makes light of the Stefan George cult. . . ." [4] And naturalism is criticized in the description of the social drama *Revenge*, which is a thinly disguised parody of Hauptmann's *Weavers*.

Today Hauptmann's play is a classic which one does not ridicule. But before accusing Heinrich Mann of poor judgment in selecting it for his attacks—he could have found many more suitable targets for his anti-naturalism—one should remember that it appeared late in the history of naturalism. Hauptmann himself was to become a neo-romantic soon after its completion. It also appeared late from the point of view of the problem presented in it.

Bismarckian legislation, while gagging the Social Democratic movement, had corrected many of the wrongs exposed in Hauptmann's masterpiece. Furthermore, the less seriously Mann took the play within his novel, the more he could stress the decadence of the spectators. The members of his sybaritic society are titillated by the sordid scenes on the stage and cheer the accusations directed against themselves, just as Schnitzler's noblemen get a thrill out of the shadows cast ahead by the French Revolution in *The Green Cockatoo.*

Heinrich Mann's Hauptmann parody is more easily defended than his shadowy hero. Bel Ami is at all times the center of the novel bearing his name. His environment comes to life because he is alive. Andreas, on the other hand, is passive and inconsistent. He lacks the strength to hold the various parts of the novel together, which, therefore, gives the effect of being disjointed and episodic. The reason for this weakness is very likely the author's desire to incorporate too many ideas, including some which he had not yet digested. In a moment of misfortune Andreas says: "Türkheimer is the power, but I am the spirit." (385) Being shallow and foolish, he is, of course, no such thing. But it will be seen that the juxtaposition of power and spirit plays an important part in many of Mann's subsequent works.

Because of its dramatically pointed dialogues and some beautiful descriptive passages, there are people who still think highly of *Im Schlaraffenland.* But it really is no more than the author's journeyman's piece, in which he tested techniques and ideas and through which he learned to write.

II *Violante*

While working on *Im Schlaraffenland,* Heinrich Mann was already collecting material for his next novel. By December, 1900, he was able to write to his publisher Langen:

Right after the completion of Capus [a translation from the French] I outlined a new novel that I am now developing. It will probably take fifteen or eighteen months. It deals with the adventures of a great lady from Dalmatia. In the first part she glows with desire for liberty; in the second, with a feeling for art; and in the third, with lust. Remarkably enough she is a human being, and is taken seriously. Most of the other figures are happy animals as in 'Schl[araffenland].' The action is dynamic. It extends to Zara, Paris, Vienna, Rome, Venice, Naples. If everything turns out well, the first part will be exotically colorful, the second art-intoxicated, and the third obscene and bitter. . . ." [5]

To this he added a few months later:

What I am doing now, sometimes seems like a modern fairy-tale to me. Please, don't be frightened. I set in motion all sorts of figures whom, in spite of their strangeness, you will find no less alive than those of my first novel. At the outset, a romantic revolution fails in a country which does not exist at all, and at the end I plan a whirl of paganism, modern swindle affairs, voluptuous artifices, classical mysteries, etc. For these, in many instances, actual affairs form the basis: Viennese court gossip, Roman [word unreadable] etc. [6]

The work appeared Christmas, 1902, with the date 1903. Its overall title was *Die Göttinnen oder Die drei Romane der Herzogin von Assy*. The names of the goddesses whom the heroine serves successively furnished the titles of the individual volumes: *Diana, Minerva,* and *Venus.*

Mann's notes to his publisher explain his intentions. He set out to explore the European phenomenon of decadence, the very decadence whose gods he had parodied in his first successful novel. For this he constructed his plot and created characters that were composites of men and women of the international set about whom he had read, but whom he himself did not know. The letters give no details concerning the characters except for the heroine, whose importance is stressed and whose progress is delineated. But the phrase "happy animals" is telling. Obviously the author had to make a conscious effort to keep an ironic distance from the figures invented by him.

In the theoretical foundation of his trilogy Mann was greatly indebted to Nietzsche, particularly, though not exclusively, to the latter's *Beyond Good and Evil* and *Toward a Genealogy of Morals.* Decadence, Nietzsche maintains, has its origin in the prevailing morality developed over two thousand years by weak but clever men who made weakness a virtue. This morality suppresses man's natural instincts and undermines his vitality. It stifles the will to act; degenerate instincts take over; pessimism conquers the mind; and instead of doing, man reflects, lives second-hand, and becomes dissatisfied. Vice, crime, perversion, resentment, envy, and hysteria are the symptoms of an age ruled by morality; and no age exhibits the signs of decay more palpably than the nineteenth century. But there exists another morality, according to the philosopher, one that is not invented by slaves, cowards, and conformists. It is the code of the "Herrenmensch," the individualist, the noble soul. It was alive in classical antiquity and had "a brilliantly-eerie reawakening" in the Renaissance. The "Herrenmensch" scorns pity, altruism, utilitarianism, and egalitarianism. He has an instinct for rank and value. Instead of meekly humbling himself, he glorifies himself. He does not long for freedom and happiness; his life *is* freedom and happiness.

Having established this ideal, Nietzsche asks himself: can a transvaluator of values like this "superman" exist in the modern world? And his answer is no. The "great health" necessary for a man to overcome the Judaeo-Christian and bourgeois notions demands a time less rotten and self-doubting than the present.

In keeping with these ideas, Mann constructed his fable, selected the proper setting and period for it, and invented artists, intellectuals, and adventurers who were conscious and articulate slaves of the cult of decadence, placing into their midst the great lady Violante, Duchess of Assy. There were many pitfalls in his method, and he did not avoid all of them, but he was successful enough to create a work that Herbert Ihering rightly calls "an almost complete document of all the addictions and fashions, all the hysterias, and artistic excesses, all the illusions and intellectual and material wastefulnesses ending in nothing, all the political and human charlataneries of the period around 1900." [7]

Nearly all the events of *Die Göttinnen* take place in the last quarter of the nineteenth century. Violante of Assy, born around 1850, enters Paris society as a very young woman, but leaves for her homeland, Dalmatia, when the Franco-Prussian War breaks out. Here she develops an interest in the conspiracy of some native peasants against their foreign king. The people's struggle reaches its high point in 1876, but the revolutionary forces are quickly subdued, and Violante has to flee. In 1880 there is a new flare-up of the insurrection which again is promptly quelled, and soon thereafter the Duchess becomes tired of the political problems of her native "goat kingdom." She moves to Venice, where in 1882 she gives her first reception. With this she abandons Diana and turns to Minerva. The second volume, dealing with her service to art, spans the next eight years, while the final volume, *Venus*, covers approximately a decade. Violante's life span, thus, is that of Nietzsche himself, and the complacent bourgeois society which she defies in fiction is identical with that which the philosopher wanted to vanquish in reality.

Violante is the aristocratic spirit incarnate. As a child she learns about her ancestors, who were warriors, grandiose barbarians, "blonde beasts." They are the ones who set her course, the only ones to whom she feels responsible. She is imbued with a strong Voltairian skepticism toward the Christian religion, and she is made to believe that she is a superior being deserving everyone's respect. After her father's death, she enters a brief, unconsummated marriage to an old uncle, thus acquiring her ducal title. When, after her husband's death, it pleases her to help liberate her countrymen, she does not act from firm political convictions, but from some vague notion of freedom and justice.

Although she soon discovers that the populace does not appreciate her idealism, she carries on as long as the preoccupation with political intrigues gives her "a sense of being alive." When it ceases to do so, she turns to art. This brings her in touch with painters, sculptors, art collectors, and poets. Some members of her fascinating circle become her friends; but friendship, admiration, and understanding never mean a true involvement or surrender on her part. Proud and aloof, she gives herself only through her beauty and radiance. Eventually even art bores her, and once more she changes her allegiance, forsaking Minerva for Venus. Carnal pleasures in a thousand forms become her passion. Orgies of lust and perversion fill the remainder of her days, gradually undermine her health, and ultimately lead to her death. In this stage, too, she retains her independence, disregards the judgment of others, and avoids permanent attachments. When self-fulfillment turns into self-destruction and the end approaches, she asks herself some searching questions: "Where is my family? To what country do I belong? To what people? To what estate? What do I represent? What community justifies me? Woe unto me if I weaken!" (706) This is followed by a frenzied and vain longing for a child. But eventually she faces death in the knowledge that her life has been right for her and worthy of her forebears.

To her environment she is at all times the "superwoman," the possessor of all inner and outer riches for which the others crave. Herr von Siebelind, who is the keenest psychologist of decadence in the novel, says of her:

Vices! The insufferable fact is that for this woman there are no vices. She lacks the concept. In advance she calls everything good that has the urge to issue from her. She believes in herself! . . . How much she has suffered: when a dream slipped away from her, when a new yearning overwhelmed her! . . . But everything suits her that creates a strong sense of vitality. Everything is a game to her, serving no other purpose than that of a beautiful gesture and a strong thrill. No intoxication carries her away forever; no misfortune can overpower her; none of all the disappointments will make her doubt life or the desirability of her own existence." (646/7)

Neither Siebelind nor anyone else sees weaknesses in the Duchess. Since she is the strongest, calmest, most composed being possible in her time, she gives the impression of being perfect. But to the reader, Heinrich Mann shows also another Violante, one that more than proves Nietzsche's dictum of the impossibility of attaining his ideal in his age.

Some signs indicating that the heroine herself is strongly affected by the disease of decadence have already been mentioned. There is first the great importance she attaches to her ancestry. Her life is determined by looking back to powerful ancestors and a glorious past. She has no real sense of freedom and acts out her existence as if it were a part in a play written long ago. She never rids herself of the feeling that "everything has been done before and seen before and painted before, every passion has been experienced, every valid action taken." [8] There is further her painful awareness of being without descendants. The strong have offspring and perpetuate themselves. Also her pursuits grow out of boredom—Siebelind euphemistically speaks of the dreams that slip away—and fragment her life into three phases, when it ought to be of one piece. And one might add another symptom not alluded to before: her inability to recognize, and make a common cause, with those who really are naïve, non-reflective, and full of a zest for life. Jakobus Halm, for instance, the painter who cannot paint beauty but only the longing for it, becomes her friend and lover. In the youth Nino, who in his high strung frailty reminds one of Hanno Buddenbrook or Conrad Ferdinand Meyer's Julian, she sees a kindred spirit. But a certain painter named Perikles, who abhors analysis, does not reflect about himself and paints out of primitive strength, is completely overlooked by her. Roger A. Nicholls sums it up well when he says that in Violante von Assy "nobility is no longer a creative self-assertion," but at best "a form of aesthetic sensibility keeping her away from the emotions of the vulgar." [9]

This list does not entirely exhaust the characteristics of Violante that make her fall short of the Renaissance ideal, but it is long enough to make one wonder why she, in spite of so much self-doubt and so many scruples, earns in her death the author's unqualified approval. The answer to this question, so it appears, can be found only in her superiority over those around her. She achieves an optimum of self-fulfillment under imperfect conditions and suffers less than the other characters of the novel from the discrepancy between her desires and her potential. A glance at the most important ones among these will clearly reveal her as the "one-eyed among the blind," and so justify her final apotheosis.

The cast of "happy animals" is as large as it is colorful. There are mysterious men like the financier Rustschuk and light opera figures like Prince Phili. There is an exiled Pasha and a toothless and greedy old principessa living in a boarding house. A blackmailing journalist has his moment of importance, as does a lady who never sleeps twice with the same man. And so one could go on almost indefinitely listing Violante's loyal servants, her ardent admirers, her enemies and competitors, and a host of others, all of whom perform a function in the economy of the novel. But the characters determining the mood of the novel and remaining of interest to Heinrich Mann in the years following the completion of the trilogy are only few: the men of action and the artists and poets.

Dr. Pavic is the leader of the Dalmatian peasant revolt. He regards himself as a hero and martyr for his ideals. He quotes the words and imitates the gestures of Christ, eventually identifying himself with Him, but in reality he is a voluble coward who feels strong only when he can spellbind an adoring crowd. In exile he becomes a parasite and derelict in whom we can take no greater interest than does the Duchess.

More sympathetic, and more honest with himself and others than Pavic, is San Bacco. A Garibaldian, this man once devoted his life and gave his fortune to his country and is still willing to wage war against tyranny of any sort. But Italy is liberated and united and the need for chivalrous soldiers is gone; only verbal fights in parliament are left for him. To teach young Nino how to fence he uses the ivory scepters of former court jesters as swords —a symbol of the anachronism which his Quixotic figure represents.

Don Saverio Cucuru,[10] the son of the toothless principessa, inherited from his mother an intense liking for wealth. His arena is neither the battlefield nor the forum; seduction is his stock-in-trade, and with the help of corrupt officials he has already acquired a number of brothels and gambling houses by the time he meets Violante. In order to make the Duchess his most expensive courtesan he holds her prisoner for some time. He also tries to obtain the power of attorney over her fabulous estate, but he fails in both endeavors. When, in a moment of love, she does offer him the power of attorney, he rejects it in favor of a passionate embrace. After that, Violante exposes him to public ridicule during a game of baccarat, and her imprisonment ends. Don Saverio, alas, proves to be no stronger than the others.

The artists in *Die Göttinnen* also exhibit weaknesses which prevent them from achieving their aims, unless, as is the case with the poetess Contessa Blà, the aim is self-annihilation. To Blà, only suffering is fulfillment, and the sadist Piselli gives perfect satisfaction to her masochism. After many extreme tortures he kills her. In her fellow artists, the destruction of the will does not go this far, but they too fail to come to terms with life. The sculptress Properzia Ponti, a woman described as huge and powerful, loves a puny little nonentity. Like Thomas Mann's Tonio Kröger, she longs for "the bliss of the commonplace"; but unlike Tonio, she finds no compromise, no *modus vivendi*, committing suicide when the unworthy object of her fiery love marries another woman. Jean Guignol—a figure inspired by the person of Gabriele D'An-

nunzio—likes to regard himself as a new Renaissance poet whose
life and poetry are in harmony with one another, but deep down
he knows that "we artists really always take revenge on everything that has inflicted wounds on our senses, that extorts yearnings from us; on the entire world." (634) And Jakobus Halm, the
painter mentioned earlier, finds a formula for the art of decadence
which is the most often quoted phrase from *Die Göttinnen.* He
calls his genre of painting "hysterical Renaissance."

Look along there. Between the old masterpieces, my own pictures
hang, and if you are of good will, you will hardly be able to pick them
out. And as for myself, as I am standing here, you can confuse me, if
you wish, with the statue of Moretto in Brescia or with that of the
great Paolo in his home town. Haha! And this masquerade gives me
my style, my much admired style! I have discovered a genre of my
own; I call it secretly: the hysterical Renaissance! Modern paucities
and perversions I dress up and put make-up on with such superior
cleverness that they seem to share in the full humanity of the golden
age. Their misery arouses no disgust but rather titillation. That is my
art! (368)

Neither the artists nor the men of action, then, can escape the
degeneracy of their age. They are marked by enervated yearnings,
egocentricities, aberrations of the mind, and frustrations resulting
from a dubious ideal. Moreover, as fictional characters in Mann's
"fairy tale" they are true mirrors of the world of reality, which
enters the hothouse atmosphere of the novel once like a gust of
cool air. Von Siebelind, this time undoubtedly the author's spokesman, has this to say about William II, Kipling, D'Annunzio, and
Nietzsche:

Who are your brothers, Nino? A monarch filled with a gnawing desire
to trample countries and whip oceans: in deepest peace he rubs his
scrofulous limbs, which easily get cold. The soldier poet of the new
Empire: blood, laurel, and tropical sun glow and soar where he strikes
his lyre, and unleashes the cries of predatory animals; but he is a
little man who cannot stand the heat in the far-flung empire of his
ideas. The magnificent poet of the most magnificent race: indefatiga-
bly he offers praise to beauty; to that beauty abounding with life
which is lying on his bed;—but his fathers sired it, and his art is a
single incest . . . And the sublime philosopher, the consummation of

millennia: he lives twenty-three and a half hours for his health in order
to jot down, in the last thirty minutes, a hymn to life. . . . (465/6)

If his work on *Die Göttinnen* had merely whetted the author's
desire further to explore the pathology of decadence and to clarify
his own attitudes, the gain would have been great enough. But
Mann also profited as a craftsman. The subject matter of his second novel was sufficiently different from that of his first to require
different stylistic devices. To be sure, there was still room for the
caricaturist; the technique of direct discourse still served useful
ends; a playlet could again be inserted and its effect on the spectators be exploited for the purpose of characterization. But additional methods were needed to describe the luxurious and artificial life of Violante and the insane ardors of many secondary
figures. These Heinrich Mann partly learned from D'Annunzio
and Hermann Hesse,[11] and in part he invented them. There is no
evidence that he knew Oscar Wilde, but a few pages are so reminiscent of Wilde's tales that one cannot rule them out as a possible
influence.

Three writing techniques well suited to the composition of a
novel of decadence seem to stand out in *Die Göttinnen*. They are
the invention of similes, for which the refined tastes of a moribund
culture furnish the imagery; the use of stark contrasts; and the
reflection of emotional states in objects surrounding the person
experiencing them. The similes are not uniquely Mann's. Images
involving candy and fragrance, silver and gold, mother of pearl
and molten stars, for instance, can be found in the works of most
writers of the so-called "esthetic movement" from Gautier to
Oscar Wilde. But the other two techniques have been accepted
and admired as influential innovations by such important poets as
Gottfried Benn and Rainer Maria Rilke.

In a tribute to Mann on the occasion of his sixtieth birthday,
Benn said, "The new art, the artistry of the post-Nietzschean
epoch, wherever it became great, was wrested from the antithesis
of intoxication and discipline." [12] His specific reference was to *Die
Göttinnen*. And Rilke wrote about Mann, "Who else has invented
landscapes so splendidly in order to have them, quite simply,
enter the blood stream of an action? This, to me, is the greatest
wonder: that someone can be the creator of forms and simultane-

ously the creator of the current that abducts them from him." [13] The use of nature—and also of artifacts—as symbols of evanescent emotional states appealed to Rilke; the use of images contrasting "intoxication" and "discipline" appealed to Benn.

Contrasts and juxtapositions abound in *Die Göttinnen*. They may appear as part of a thought: "They saw the voluptuous wives of the sultan writhe, and remembered a chaste child with firmly closed mouth who was waiting at home." (12) They may occur as a change of action and locale: "She came from a colorful still life [a harem] where under passionate sighs and the clanking of daggers commands were issued to beautifully gowned slaves. Immediately thereafter she intended to teach freedom to a ragged mob and involve them in a revolution." (90) Or it may serve, sometimes with wry humor, to characterize minor figures: "They seemed to belong to a sort of men who through their *savoir faire* adorn every salon, and whom one considers capable, in a critical hour, after a gambling loss, of tearing off the bejeweled ear lobes of women." (43/44)

It is a case of the imagination bridling the imagination. The raging intensities of *Die Göttinnen*—Benn's "intoxication"—chasing one another throughout the novel, would become unbearable to the reader without balancing counter-images. In a few instances where the controlling half, the "discipline," is either lacking or ill-conceived, Mann's style tends to evoke laughter. The description of Properzia Ponti is a case in point. "Properzia was a striding powerful block of marble. Her hands wrestled with other blocks. In this head the thoughts had to be inscribed on marble slabs in strong lettering. And a smooth little dwarf, smiling skeptically, scratched his name on them." (181) Here the marble image is overdone and by no means set in perspective by the reference to Properzia's puny lover. Instead of a "female Michelangelo," [14] a mountain of a woman emerges. And a later mention of her "wall of black hair" (318) does not help matters at all. Such lapses are fortunately not too frequent, but they show the dangers inherent in Mann's supercharged language.

Rilke's remarks must allude to passages in *Die Göttinnen* like the following. "Her grief, hardened by day by a thousand hammer strokes, dissolved in the May evening; it spread over the sky with the glow of the sun, ran down the dunes with the sand, dispersed in idle chatter like any wave on the beach." (332) This sentence, which in German possesses a most appropriate rhythm and the support of a fine distribution of various vowel sounds, is truly evocative. Even more poetic is an example in which a work of art takes the place of a nature image and gains the quality of a real symbol. At one point the author describes a gallery, at the two ends of which two white marble figures rise from a green background, "a boy over here, and at the other end a girl. They smiled and placed a finger to their mouths." (109) Eight pages later, a young woman, whom her mother has forced to become the mistress of an uncouth clergyman, is asked by the latter to sing. Slowly she walks to the end of the gallery. "There she stopped and sang something. One saw her indistinctly. Her voice slipped through the room frightened as if choked by the shadows. The shimmering figure of the marble boy behind her placed a finger to his mouth." This is reminiscent of Rilke's own manner, as, for instance, in the poem "Letzter Abend" from the year 1906, in which a shako with a death's head emblem symbolizes the moment when the meaning of a departure is realized. In *Die Göttinnen,* the roguish gesture of the marble figure suddenly assumes a variety of meanings exceeding the simple equation of an allegory.

Rilke and Benn were not the only ones to admire *Die Göttinnen.* As late as 1961, Kasimir Edschmid acknowledged the importance of this work as a treasure trove for expressionists by saying:

About Heinrich Mann I had written in 1920, in my *Die doppelköpfige Nymphe,* that the young people always mentioned his name with reverence. He was beacon and strength in the most desolate times. One will not cease to bow before the 'Duchess of Assy', to sense the sweetness and *marches funèbres* of such proud self-awareness. Someone angrily scourged the era here, from a distance and with discipline, and yet pointed out to it the beauty of the islands, of the ships, of bravery, out of the depth of history. The excesses of the mind found no more shining hero.[15]

In a lengthy study dealing exclusively with *Die Göttinnen,* many more facets of Mann's style could be discussed. Here it is enough to point out that in writing this very ambitious work he widened his range enormously, going the whole gamut from brilliant displays of verbal fireworks to the muted tones of finest lyricism. That he did so without complete surety has already been pointed out. Yet not the stylistic weaknesses, but rather the unconvincingly developed idea of "pagan sensuality" and the static and contradictory figure of the heroine prevented the book from becoming more than an inspiration for other writers and a second proving-ground for its author. He was to do better soon.

CHAPTER 3

The First Edifice

I *The Weak and the Strong*

AFTER the completion of *Die Göttinnen* Heinrich Mann wrote with speed and ease. In 1903 he also published *Die Jagd nach Liebe,* which was followed at two-year intervals by three additional novels: *Professor Unrat* in 1905, *Zwischen den Rassen* in 1907, and *Die kleine Stadt* in 1909. Simultaneously a score of novellas and short stories appeared in print—a truly astonishing output. Naturally, there were differences in quality, but so many of Mann's enduring works belong to what has been called his "first period of creativity" that he would have to be regarded as an important author even if, at the age of forty, he had completely ceased to write.

Like its predecessor, *Die Jagd nach Liebe* is a novel of decadence, though "not a Renaissanceistic one," as Weisstein puts it.[1] Its locale is Munich, its time is around 1900, and it is populated by "sons and grandsons with whose exhausted vitality their once vigorous families expire."[2] There is little attempt on the part of any character to pursue a positive goal. There is no figure possessed of a sense of social responsibility. The southern German world of the *art nouveau* era depicted in *Die Jagd nach Liebe* is condemned by the author as sterile, empty, and worthless.

The first critics, part and parcel of the society portrayed, heartily disliked the book. "The press was irritated rather than cool."[3] Insofar as they objected to its loose structure, they had a point. The novel was written in about six months and shows the haste of its composition. But as regards the characters and ideas they were wrong. Mann rightly took exception to the opinion that his work was "simply another effusion of sensuality."[4] For with the figures of Ute Ende and Panier, and with the recognition of the year 1870 as a dividing line between a healthy and a diseased Germany, he had taken a big step forward in the clarification of his own thoughts.

Ute Ende is an actress who experiences the loneliness and isolation of the artist. The world seems crude and insensitive to her. But in contrast to the poet Jean Guignol, remembered from *Die Göttinnen*, she does not really try to find a link with "life." Her art absorbs her fully. She is without feeling and incapable of love, and one wonders whether her acting is a compensation for her inability to be a person, or whether she was born a normal woman whose art has drained her of all genuine emotions. At any rate, she exists only as an actress. Claude Marehn, her decadent lover, knows this when he says:

That means that you want to be a work of art and no longer a human being. Don't you people always carry your works of art around with you? Doesn't one always see them in your face? You yourselves are your work. Out of yourselves, your bodies, your souls, you make a work of art, composed of chest sounds and shrieking, of make-up, of silk on cardboard, of solemnly swaying steps, of—I don't know what.[5]

Ute is one of a number of performing artists created by Mann, who, being completely devoured by their art, become as obsessed with power within their sphere as any despot can possibly be in the realm of political life. One of these in particular will be scrutinized carefully below so that at present no more needs to be said about this fascinating type.

Panier is a man with "broad shoulders and ruthless elbows" whose interests are limited to money and women. Because of this he reminds one at first of characters like Türkheimer and Cucuru, but it is not to these that he is related. He made his money through the work of his hands, has real courage, and exhibits strength even when he joins in with the sybaritism of the society around him. Nothing about him is a pose. In a working copy of *Die Jagd nach Liebe*, an entry, probably made by Mann for a lecture, refers to Panier as "an old gent out of more vigorous times." This is a clue that Panier must be regarded as the German counterpart to the Garibaldian San Bacco, who also possesses a healthy energy which the younger generation cannot muster.

The "more vigorous times" do not lie very far in the past. For

Heinrich Mann their end came in Germany with the Franco-Prussian War—the event that also brought about the unification of Italy. In a conversation between Ute Ende and her friend Bella, the old breed of men is compared to the new as follows:

After all, we are not dealing with the type of nervy bumpkin who went through the War of 1870 and who makes his wife happy by giving her babies to put on the pottie and lamps to clean. The type of today is weaker than we; he cries for a female companion . . . for a woman to save him from his nihilistic loneliness.[6]

Here for the first time the Age of Bismarck is played out against the Age of William II—a theme that Heinrich Mann touched upon frequently in his second period, when he devoted himself almost exclusively to a critique of the Kaiser and his Reich.

In the spring of 1903, Heinrich Mann interrupted his work on *Die Jagd nach Liebe* in order to write his best known novella, "Pippo Spano."[7] This tale strikes one as an afterthought to *Die Göttinnen*, but an afterthought of such brilliance and beauty that it overshadows, as a work of art, the ambitious trilogy out of which it grew.

The central idea of "Pippo Spano" is the gulf between art and life, as experienced by a poet and playwright who carries his "Renaissance cult" to its ultimate conclusion and thereby reveals its absurdity. It illustrates Nietzsche's aphorism that artists are not men of passion but exploiters of passion. At the same time it reveals the non-artists, whom they wish to emulate, as much weaker than they appear to their impotent admirers.

The poet Mario Malvolto believes that "war and art are both the same super-human exaggerations." Therefore he keeps in his study the picture of the condottiere Pippo Spano. The portrait of this dynamic individual painted by the quattrocento painter Andrea del Castagno is to function as his guide and conscience. Malvolto is one of the "inadequate late-born ones," who wishes to create for himself through art "a second, more powerful life." "Life" suddenly comes to him in the person of young Gemma Cantoggi, who offers him her love. Pippo Spano's smile tells him that he must accept her or forever renounce the world of the strong. Malvolto chooses love and is willing to give up writing. But one day Gemma informs her lover that their secret is betrayed and that only death is left for them. Now Malvolto realizes that he does not possess the fortitude necessary to justify his choice. On the stage characters can die heroically, but one does not do so in real life. He goes so far as to kill Gemma, but her death drains him of the strength to commit suicide. The scornful grin of the portrait on the wall makes it clear to him that he still is what he always was, namely, an artist and not a man of action. He stands there despairing, annihilated, "an actor on whom the curtain forgot to fall."

Malvolto is Jean Guignol-D'Annunzio *redivivus,* but this time truly the *Grand Guignol,* the clown. In *Die Göttinnen,* the poet ends his life because he cannot reach the ideal represented by Violante von Assy. Malvolto, however, is not capable of such a deed. He is a narrow-chested onlooker with impotent yearnings who cannot cross over into the realm of life. Furthermore he has a false image of that realm. Those whom he admires do not possess the qualities which he ascribes to them. Gemma tells him this when she mentions the fact that her former fiancé Lanti uses artificial stimuli to appear more masculine than he really is. But Malvolto regards even the weakest non-artist as a fitting object of envy, carrying the Nietzschean adoration of strength to ridiculous excess. He therefore is bound to reach an impasse.

The key sentence in the novella appears to be the one linking war and art as "super-human exaggerations." It recurs in a significant variation when Malvolto explains to Gemma that art, war, and power are "unnatural excesses which demand a man in his entirety." Here it is brought out that war and art, irreconcilable as they may be, obey the same laws. Not only Pippo Spano, but also his painter, who is never mentioned by name, appears as a ruthless individual. Mario Malvolto's insane aspirations are, in part at least, predicated on the idea that artists potentially possess the amoral vigor of generals. In art, as in life,—and war appertains to life—the only driving force is a quest for power. Heinrich Mann demonstrates that, unless compromises are made, this quest leads to despotism. And unbridled despotism, seemingly enhancing one's "sense of vitality," defeats its purpose in the end and leads to the destruction of the self.

In 1948 Mann had occasion to point to "Pippo Spano" as a possible touchstone for people's *Weltanschauungen*. "Later," he wrote, "there existed indeed a type that soon was to be called fascist. A stranger who probably had a good education wrote: 'One novella of yours I loved.' I immediately conjectured: 'Pippo Spano', and I conjectured: a fascist who merely fails to notice that the would-be Pippo collapses miserably." [8]

"Pippo Spano" was not printed until 1905, hence appearing almost simultaneously with Mann's first truly enduring full-length novel: *Professor Unrat*. In this work, too, the main theme is the Nietzschean Will-to-Power, the intoxication that comes with its possession, and the final self-destruction of those addicted to it. But even better than before, Mann succeeded in telling a gripping tale without "laboured subtlety," as his translator says;[9] a story in which the setting becomes a living force of antagonism against the hero; and in which the hero himself is a maniac who nevertheless earns our compassion.

Three factors make *Professor Unrat* an outstanding work. First, Mann selected for his locale his native town of Lübeck. Every page betrays an intimate knowledge of streets and people that is missing from his earlier descriptions of Berlin or of cosmopolitan societies. Secondly, he did not need to strain his imagination to bring his main character to life, for Unrat represents a type of man the brothers Mann knew at first hand.[10] And thirdly, he had learned something about love that he could pass on to his fictional professor, giving him the dimensions of a truly tragic figure. "It is quite understandable to me," he wrote to a girl friend, "that you esteem 'Unrat' more highly than the Duchess. . . . 'Unrat,' this ridiculous old ogre, at least feels love for the 'Artist' Fröhlich, defends her against the whole world, and heaps upon her all his wounded tenderness. He is therefore more human than the Duchess; therefore you understand him better." [11]

In a brief essay, "Der blaue Engel wird mir vorgeführt" ("The Blue Angel is shown to me") Mann tells how he came to write the book. "I first learned of the things that happen in it while I was sitting in a theater in Florence. During the intermission, a newspaper was sold in the house; in it I found a report from Berlin about a professor whose relations to a lady from the cabaret had led him criminally astray." [12] The report turned out to be vague and ambiguous. The professor was no real professor.[13] And so, as is often the case, a misunderstanding became the source of inspiration, first for a superb narrative and, twenty-five years later, for an important film.

The film *The Blue Angel*, which also established the fame of Marlene Dietrich, made Heinrich Mann's name a household word in Europe. In 1931, in France, "l'auteur le L'Ange bleu" was given an honored seat at the table of Maréchal Liautey,[14] and when the Third Reich began, he was considered so well known a representative of democracy that a jumping-jack with the author's head and Marlene's legs was in great demand among the Nazis and their followers.[15] In the United States the film was also successful, but Mann was not identified with it. If one mentions him today as the originator of the story on which the film is based, people usually express surprise.

Carl Zuckmayer's screen adaptation follows Mann's story fairly closely, but supplies a significantly different ending. The film, in the classical tradition, allows the professor-turned-clown to go back to his old schoolhouse and die a broken man. The sounds of a song that function as a leitmotiv assigned to him, "Üb immer Treu und Redlichkeit" ("Always Practice Loyalty and Integrity") indicate that he is aware of his wrongs and failures. In a much more modern way, Heinrich Mann does not endow his sick hero with a conscience, as Schiller, for instance, might have done. Instead of a man who gains a moment's insight into the nature of his failings, we see a raving paranoiac mocked by the public as he is taken to jail.

But let us begin by briefly sketching the outlines of the rather simple plot. Professor Raat, called "Unrat" (refuse, filth) by nearly everyone, hates his students, whose juvenile jokes and pranks he takes to be an attack against his person and authority. Three of them in particular he wishes to destroy: the young nobleman Count Ertzum, the worker's son Kieselack, and the patrician Lohmann. Lohmann seems to be his worst foe, since he neither fears nor hates his teacher but merely observes and pities him. When the three teenagers repeatedly visit a cheap burlesque house where the "artist" Rose Fröhlich performs, Unrat sees his chance "to catch" them. He follows them, meets Rosa, is drawn to her, returns frequently, and eventually marries her.

He loses his job, spends his savings, and finally hosts wild parties and gambling sessions to support his family. That is to say, ostensibly he endeavors to make a living in this way; but to catch people, to ruin respectable citizens—all rebels against his rule and many of them former students of his—appears to be of far greater importance to him than the precarious existence he manages to eke out. As he sinks lower and lower, he more and more condones his wife's philanderings which yield new victims constantly. Only Lohmann, the professor-pimp insists, must not enjoy her favors. And so, when the young man, after a long stay abroad, pays Miss Fröhlich an innocent visit, the professor goes berserk, nearly kills his wife, whom he really loves, and steals the visitor's purse. The police carry off the crazed pathetic remnants of a man, and with him the girl who was his glory and his undoing.

Those familiar with the many theories about the German novella will have gathered from the foregoing that *Professor Unrat* belongs as much to this genre as it does to that of the novel. A new and unheard of event gleaned from a newspaper entry is its nucleus. The main character does not gradually develop but is suddenly revealed. His natural inclinations, barely repressed by convention at the beginning, break through after the "turning point," which is marked by the entrance of Rosa Fröhlich into his life. Even a central symbol can be found for the ambiguity of Unrat's existence—a "falcon," as it is often called because of Heyse's theory, which sets up Boccaccio's tale about Federigo and his falcon as a model.[16] In the novel, that falcon is Unrat's language, about which more will be said later. Only its length, then, and the byplay concerning secondary characters, make Mann's story a genuine novel.[17]

A teacher, and especially a Gymnasium teacher of Latin, Greek, and German, was a most felicitous choice for the type of man Heinrich Mann wished to portray. Teachers in general are people whose education develops in them tastes and levels of aspiration that exceed their social and economic status. Their position of authority is an ambiguous one. Within the classroom they are the masters, but the students know that school is only part of life, and they bring their outside lives into the classroom. They have homes and spare-time, and some day every one of them leaves his alma mater. And so their respect and deference has something of a game about it. One of the rules of the game is that it must be played with absolute seriousness—which is apt to be confusing to the teacher—but a game it remains, nevertheless.

Unrat, the German Gymnasium professor with full academic training in the classics, does not accept the discrepancy between appearance and reality. He plays a king on the stage represented by the school; a ruler who defends law and order. But his pupils play double roles. They are fellow actors and, at the same time, spectators. This is a source of annoyance to him. And the fact that the town does not support his claims to authority, he accepts as proof of its depravity. That is why he must exploit whatever means the rules of the game afford him; he must "catch" the students, "impede their careers," stop them from "achieving the goal of the class," and be "a hindrance in their lives."

But, alas, the old school martinet with his sly and vindictive eyes, wooden chin, and knock-kneed legs has an uneasy conscience. He does not really believe in the order he professes to safeguard or to incarnate. To Rosa he explains,

It is, in sooth, well known to me, that so-called morality is, generally, most intimately linked with stupidity. Only a person without human-istic education can doubt this. Yet, morality has an advantage for those who, not having it, can easily dominate those who cannot do without it. One might even assert and prove that so-called morality must be resolutely demanded from subaltern souls. This demand, how-ever,—note well, now!—has never misled me to recognize that there may be other circles with moral laws quite different from those of the average Philistine. (565)

In the past, he admits, he has had no occasion to apply such a "master race" philosophy to himself, therefore abiding by com-mon petty bourgeois standards. But when Rosa furnishes a reason, he defends himself before his principal by saying, "Sir, the Athe-nian Pericles had, in sooth, Aspasia for a mistress." (541)

Defender of a faith he does not possess, he fights for it in the same way that Thomas Mann's Gustav Aschenbach writes his masterpieces, namely *à rebours.* Once in the orbit of Rosa

Fröhlich he surrenders to degradation and chaos, as Aschenbach surrenders to Venice and Tadzio.[18] But there are important differences between the two. Aschenbach's "heroism born of weakness" consists in his faithful and disciplined manner of writing literary masterpieces. It is his professional use of words that earns him the respect of the world. When he succumbs to the lure of beauty and death, he ceases to write. Unrat, on the other hand, betrays his fundamentally anti-social attitude exactly by his awkward way of using words. Also, Unrat's dissolution is not a private matter, as is that of Thomas Mann's hero, but a public phenomenon which involves Rosa and many of the inhabitants of the town.

Unrat has no language of his own. Nothing he says corresponds directly and authentically to the thoughts he expresses. Though he has lived more than a quarter of a century in the city by the sea, he has never mastered its low German dialect and cannot really communicate with the people. Nor does he use a standard speech that might identify him with another place or social class. From cumbersomely literal translations of Homer he has borrowed obsolete and stilted phrases, which he mixes with the expletives of a pedantic schoolman, and, in moments of excitement, with student jargon. For example, many dictionaries do not contain the word *kabuff*. It is a term used by uneducated people in some German regions to designate a closet or sometimes a toilet. The slang term "can" for the latter approximates its level. Unrat uses it to refer to the students' coat closet, and the first mention of it illustrates the complete incongruity of the professor's diction: "You are not worthy of whetting your witless pen on the sublime figure of the Maid of Orleans whom we shall now discuss. Away with you to the can." The people in Unrat's environment recognize him as alien, but dismiss his linguistic idiosyncrasies with amusement. They do not realize that the character who has no language has lost touch with, and faith in, any kind of reality. Only Lohmann, at first merely embarrassed by the crazy-quilt speech pattern of the "wooden clown," subsequently discovers its meaning.

Unrat's love for Rosa is the key to the sympathy we feel for him, as Heinrich Mann correctly understood. Unlike Tadzio, Rosa is more than a symbol, a Hermes figure, or a messenger of Eros; she is a person. That she is a woman endowed with a naïve shrewdness complicates matters even more. This shrewdness, increased by a

hard life, makes her seek out older men of the fatherly type. When
she is bound to Unrat, her naïveté allows her to become a willing
tool in the hands of her husband without finding her new role
problematical. At first, the bombastic schoolmaster appears as a
shy little boy in her presence. He must be led every step of the
way toward the eventual marriage. His belated sensuality is a torture to him that does not end until he fully accepts responsibility
for Rosa and her child. Once he does accept it, he finds himself
deeply in love; and now new agonies await him, for the tender
husband and stepfather is soon placed in a position where he
needs his wife to attract wealthy members of the community to
the orgies on which the family must live. And the horrible thing is
that he enjoys Rosa's and his own degradation, since in this way
he can punish the citizens who have ostracized him, and drag
down with him those who have failed to accept his authority.
Lohmann analyzes Unrat's mind for Rosa accurately when he
says:

He is the tyrant who would rather perish than endure the limitation
of his power. A mocking word—and such words still penetrate at night
through the purple draperies of his bed and into his dream—causes
blue spots to appear on his skin. And to recover from these he needs
a blood bath. He is the inventor of lèse majesty. He would invent it
if necessary . . . . Misanthropy becomes a gnawing torture to him.
It fills his entrails with a need for revenge; it stretches his nerves to
the snapping point that there are lungs around him which inhale and
exhale without his having regulated their breath. It only takes an
impetus, a chance recalcitrance of circumstances . . . it only takes
the over-irritation of his natural predispositions and drives, for example
through a woman—and the tyrant, seized by panic, calls the mob in
the palace, incites them to arson, proclaims anarchy. (613)

Lohmann does not sufficiently stress, however, that this particular
tyrant has problems because of his genuine affection for Rosa.
Therefore the omniscient author tells the reader directly:

She was the obverse of his passion: she had to receive everything
to the degree that the other lost everything. . . . His overstimulated
impulse of tenderness had been directed toward her. That was bad
for Unrat: he told himself so. He told himself that the "artist" Fröhlich
should have been nothing but an instrument to "catch" his students

and to get them into trouble. Instead of that, she stood next to him on his level, elevated and sacred in the face of humanity, and he was compelled to love her and to suffer from his love which rebelled against the service of hatred. (600)

And we believe what Lohmann does not fully grasp, namely that Unrat's suffering from his unsolvable conflict can only end in madness or death.

With the words "tyrant" and "anarchy" Lohmann points to the socio-political implications of Unrat's surrender to the dark forces of formlessness. But the intellectual Lohmann doubts his own analysis, believing "merely to exaggerate an abstract possibility." Only when he himself becomes Unrat's victim does he realize both the accuracy of his appraisal and the true import of the events which he is witnessing. This happens soon after he has made the keen observation quoted above. On Rosa's invitation he visits Unrat's house, when suddenly the old professor appears, loses the last remnants of composure, attempts to choke his wife, and steals Lohmann's wallet. This has a startling effect on the onlooker and commentator. "Lohmann's mind, which never had been tested on such incredible experiences, cast off all individuality and responded to "crime" in the best bourgeois manner with 'police!'"

Professor Unrat is viewed here as a work dealing with two basic problems, namely the Lohmann problem, which is that of the attitude of the intellect toward power and violence, and the Unrat problem, which is that of the relationship of despotism to decadence. The former is further explored in Mann's next novel of the year 1907, *Zwischen den Rassen;* the latter constitutes the central theme of two novellas published in 1908, namely "Die Branzilla" and "Der Tyrann." But Hermann Sinsheimer and Herbert Ihering are perfectly correct in also stressing two other aspects of *Professor Unrat.* Sinsheimer sees the essence of this work in the impact which Unrat has upon the town.

In the little town, people live lives appropriate to the town. . . . Everything about them and their lives remains petty, clean, and, by the by, a bit embarrassing. With their unprepossessing virtues and vices they have room in the little belly of the town. But Unrat steps among them, a fellow stirred up by the grammar and the dubiousness of a larger world; someone banished into the little town, a stranger, then, and an enemy of the town.

This sociological motive . . . gives the action its great upsurge. From the beginning, Unrat is not only a sardonic philologist but an Attila, a scourge, a phantom raised into the unreal before whose being the town trembles in its foundations.[19]

And Ihering remarks: *"Professor Unrat* is the first work by Heinrich Mann which undermines one of the pillars of power of Wilhelminian Germany, namely the school."[20] Both Sinsheimer and Ihering bring to their approaches their knowledge of Heinrich Mann's later development, anticipating works like *Die kleine Stadt* and *Der Untertan.* They are quoted here primarily to show the richness of a novel that is not readily exhausted by a single reading or a brief discussion.

II *Toward Democracy*

Zwischen den Rassen is not as important a novel as its predecessor. Although it contains many beautiful passages and anticipates the ideology of the later Heinrich Mann, it can hardly be called a major work, for it is too much of an incongruous mixture. Autobiographical elements and political theories, aspects of the *Bildungsroman* and backstage sensationalism, sublimely lyrical passages and touches of the picaresque may all be found in it. Its significance therefore rests in the role it plays in the author's personal development.

As in *Die Göttinnen,* Mann chose a woman for his central figure. This afforded him the opportunity to make full use of the story of his mother's childhood,[21] furnishing with her ethnic background—which of course is also his—the basis for her outlook on life. Furthermore, by making the heart of his heroine the primary battleground for the struggle between life and intellect, the author could exploit fully the erotic side of his problem. The infatuation of an intelligent woman with a robust superman is perfectly plausible. On the other hand, a woman cannot completely express the masculine author's point of view. And so Heinrich Mann created a triangle, placing Lola Gabriel between the anti-intellectual Count Pardi and the writer Arnold Acton, the latter being as much Mann's alter ego as is Lola.

Lola Gabriel, the daughter of a German father and a Brazilian mother, born at the edge of the virgin forest of South America, is taken by Mr. Gabriel to Germany for her education. The change has a traumatic effect on the child. She feels at home nowhere—a girl without a country, different from other children. She feels that her father has betrayed her and becomes suspicious and distrustful. This trait she retains almost to the end of her story. Even when she knows to whom her heart truly belongs she says, "I understand that women of my type promise themselves to Christ. They could trust no one but Him." (397) And only her final statement of love, the last sentence of the book, evinces a healing of the injury caused by her removal from her native environment.

Lola's Germanic and Latin blood [22] places her outside any existing society. Her fate is that of Tonio Kröger, whose duality is shown even in his name. But suspicious Lola cannot rise to the Thomas Mannian irony. Irony, the "pathos of the middle," [23] represents not only a central position between two opposites, but also a superior one with regard to both. Superiority is incompatible with distrust. There is no way for Lola to rise above her conflicts. They must be fought out within her, fully and seriously.

Her path leads her from Northern Germany to Spain, Bavaria, and Italy. In Bavaria she meets the two men between whom she must choose: Arnold Acton, the German poet and dreamer who abhors violence, and Cesare Augusto Pardi, the robust Italian man of action. The choice is a difficult one. Pardi's sinewy strength is appealing. His direct manner of courting flatters her. His certainty of conquest is overwhelming. Compared to him, Arnold looks unmanly. But Arnold has kindness and decency on his side. It is a shame that "only weakness brings forth intellect and kindness depends on cognition." (127) After many agonizing debates with herself, Lola allows her senses to win out over reason: she marries Pardi.

Lola's choice corresponds, so it seems, to the author's own admiration of Nietzsche. Therefore it is only natural that, by way of an apology, Mann stresses the seductive qualities of his scoundrel. Pardi is selfish and ruthless, to be sure. But he is also convinced of the rightness of his views, which happen to benefit only him. His statements possess a grandiose sweep which tends to convince the characters to whom they are addressed, and also to impress the reader of the novel. For instance, when he has lost Lola's affection and becomes jealous of Acton he says:

There are women who were great in their betrayal. La Cupola, to save her husband, did this, too; she sold herself. Oh! Your high self-esteem would have forbidden you this, I know. How could you demean yourself and serve? Are you a woman like our women? But I swear to you: like ours you could have had ten lovers and still be my wife; I should have hunted you and brought you down; but then I should have wept on your coffin for love. And now I shall spit on it. (421)

Such explosions sound majestic and honest, and it takes a moment's thought on the part of the reader before Pardi's arrogance becomes apparent.

But the fascination exercised by Pardi over the woman in Lola—that is to say, by primitive force over the mind—does not by itself account for her becoming Pardi's wife. From her earliest years, Lola Gabriel has painfully recognized that she is without roots and looked for a substitute for home. In her first aimless travels, art offers her a temporary refuge. The best bel canto singer of her time, La Branzilla, trains her voice and she submits willingly to the tyranny of her teacher who, herself, has risen to the pinnacle of artistic perfection and fame by subordinating her humanity to art. But La Branzilla goes mad and leaves Lola incapable of carrying on by herself. "Branzilla's method left one dependent to the end. Lola was powerless without her leader. The road to art, this new home, was lost." (100) The result is a vacuum in Lola's existence which Pardi is just the man to fill. The despot of life supplants Branzilla, the despot of art.

The marriage to Pardi proves to be one prolonged series of agonies. Lola loves him in her way; she admires the he-man; she surrenders as completely as she can. At the same time, her super-ego is wide awake, observing and criticizing herself and Pardi. She rebels against the endless series of humiliations which she has to endure and yet realizes that only she is responsible for them. The more her self-respect is undermined, the clearer it becomes to her that all guilt is hers and not that of her "accessory."

What is her guilt, and why is it that Pardi does not share it? Admittedly, she betrayed herself to the flesh. She did so in the belief that she could win him over to what she calls "higher humanity"; but she should have known that this is impossible.

Before our marriage he was the same, and I knew it. I knew he was brutal, a scoundrel, and incapable of justice. All this was transfigured, almost spiritualized by a sort of heroism; by a grandiose vanity and readiness to stand up with his whole personality for any trifle. . . . He is not the one who is guilty. He would have satisfied many another woman, many of those unconscious creatures whom he resembles. The responsibility rests with me. I looked ahead. (306)

The primitive brute is no more to be blamed than the predatory felines with whom Pardi is compared in numerous similes and metaphors.[24] But she, Lola, who responds to the male desires evoked by her beauty, also has a mind. In her is some of the independence—and also some of the sterility—of the Duchess of Assy. Her guilt stems from her awareness. When awareness makes itself subservient to instinct, it pronounces its own condemnation.

In his optimism the author wills it that Lola's sufferings have an end. While the barbarian cannot be won for "higher humanity," the intellectual can be made to cross over into the realm of action.[25] Arnold Acton, who despises all heroics, who refuses to compete for Lola's love, and who even abstains from possessing her after she has professed her love for him, challenges Pardi to a duel when he believes him to have harmed Lola physically. The challenge, anticipated by Acton's early statement that he might use violence if there were someone "who must not live any longer" (183), is the moment of Lola's and Arnold's rebirth. As the intellect resorts to force in behalf of the intellect, mind and body are reunited. The intellect is not corrupted thereby since force remains its servant.

The duel, of course, stands for action as such, but in particular for resistance to tyranny. As a woman, Lola can experience the erotic but she cannot fight the ideological battle as well as a man can fight it. This is one of Arnold Acton's tasks. The German poet with the English name—perhaps borrowed from Lord Dalberg-Acton[26] or perhaps merely used because of its phonetic closeness to the word "action"—undergoes a change similar to that of the woman he loves, gradually learning that men of the mind cannot completely withdraw from the arena of life. A harmony, preestablished by Heinrich Mann, brings about the coincidence of Lola's nadir with Acton's challenge.

Another one of Acton's functions is that of being the author's spokesman. It is in Acton's pronouncements, rather than in Lola's, that Mann makes clear what will occupy his mind after the completion of this novel. Having dismissed his aristocratic ideals, he will describe life in an essentially democratic society and, Pardi notwithstanding, this will be an Italian society. Acton says:

. . . In this sociable race, possessing a sense for public phenomena, public freedom remains always more important than private freedom. We Germans, poorer in political rights than any other people of Europe, like to console ourselves with our inner freedom. What is it to us that in the crude world of phenomena we have masters, since inwardly we are past all that and everyone by himself in his four walls is a little king or even a big one. But the people here are rarely in their four walls. They descend to the plazas, talk simultaneously, think in common and by chain reaction, and, like real young people who still live by reason and vision, know no difference between inner and outer experience. (354)

And from this he draws the conclusion that the people of the north, about to perish through rationalization, will have to be rejuvenated with the help of those of the south whose "healthier animality has saved them from the seduction and vices of the intellect." (355) These statements furnish the ideological link between *Zwischen den Rassen* and Mann's next novel, *Die kleine Stadt;* between the final abandonment of Nietzschean concepts and the acceptance of a democratic philosophy.

Before addressing oneself to Mann's next and most nearly perfect novel, however, one does well to consider two novellas which in 1908 appeared together under the title *Die Bösen* ("The Evil Ones") and which may be regarded as stylistic exercises in preparation for the masterpiece. I am referring to "Die Branzilla" and "Der Tyrann."

"Der Tyrann" tells of a nineteenth century Italian duke who has a beautiful woman brought to his chambers ostensibly in order to make love to her. She, however, comes to kill him. Her motives are two: she is devoted to the cause of freedom, and she yearns to avenge the assassination of her brother. The Duke talks gently to her, listens to her moving plea for political reform and acts as if he were swayed by her arguments. When eventually he declares himself willing to abdicate, the woman's hatred changes to admiration, and she reveals her original intention. At this point he admits that he was only toying with her. The story ends with his calling the guards, who take her to the executioner while he turns his back.

The Duke is a decadent. He has long known Raminga Guidati and should like to possess her. But love would destroy his isolation and render him incapable of further ruthlessness. This is an unbearable thought to him who realizes that he is nothing without power. "He who knows the uniqueness of the tyrant," he says, "his way of toying with human beings, his disdain for humanity, his fear of men—do not for a moment believe that he will voluntarily renounce it." His strong ancestors could rule without fear. They did not inherit their power; they acquired it, and lustily wielded it without compunction. For the weakling Alessandro there remains only a perverted sense of pride in a greatness stemming from his very weakness. "Does not a person deserve greater respect who, not brave by nature, forces himself to act as if he were!" he exclaims. There is no way for Raminga to reach him. She goes to her death disillusioned and horrified.

But more interesting than the psychology of decadence, often explored by Mann, is the technique of "Der Tyrann." At its beginning the scene is set. The Duke is allowed an expository monologue; and from then on the story consists almost entirely of dialogue. The speeches are interrupted only by a few sentences describing gestures, noises, and the entrance and exit of guards; in other words, by stage directions.

"Der Tyrann" was indeed performed as a one-act play. Karl Strecker, who reviewed both the novella and the stage version, liked the former better, but while reading it he was constantly reminded of the latter.[27] His reactions were proper, and his observations astute. The fifty-eight changes made for the theater appear necessary in part and are largely minor; but some passages were eliminated from the story for the sake of a fast-paced performance that sinks deep shafts into the complex character of the Duke. Hence, as a psychological study the novella is better than the drama. On the other hand, good actors originally created the roles of the Duke and Raminga, and good actors can add nuances to a script which in recollection enhances the plasticity of a narrative.

The inner tensions of the Duke, his love-hate for Raminga, and his moment of conflict while vice and virtue lure him equally, justify the dramatic form of the story. Yet the almost exclusive use of direct discourse in the story would not be possible if "Der Tyrann" were dealing with more than a single brief episode in the sad career of its protagonist. When an entire life is to be encompassed and terseness is nevertheless desired, other techniques must be used, such as are found in "Die Branzilla."

"Die Branzilla" concerns the bel canto singer who is already known by the reader as Lola Gabriel's teacher. Her problem is similar to that of Alessandro. She is as autocratic an artist as he is a ruler. Mann does not make a difference between the various spheres of life in which people tyrannize others while being themselves tyrannized by their compulsions. The Duke reveals the bond between him and Branzilla, when he says, "I am an artist, Signora, more than you think." La Branzilla is an artist and might as well say, "I am a despot."

Her life is presented in seven chapters, each of which deals with a crucial phase of it. As a young girl she sings at a private gathering and gains a sponsor in the wealthy Dario Rupa. Five years later a revolution breaks out, and Rupa is thought guilty of conspiracy. He is not, but Branzilla testifies to his guilt in order to stay in the good graces of the government and to avoid having her career interrupted, if not ended. Once she has become a highly reputed singer, she poisons La Amati, the only rival who stands between her and the pinnacle of success. A hunchbacked singer named Sturbanotte is witness to the murder, but cannot bring her to justice. In the fourth chapter, Cavazzaro appears. He is a man with an excellent voice and a tremendous zest for life. Branzilla falls in love and marries him. It does not take long until the incompatibility of the couple becomes apparent. Cavazzaro can drink to excess and make love to many women without detriment to his art, whereas Branzilla lives like a nun to achieve perfection in her performances. In spite of her obsessions, however, she shows good insight into her character in chapter six, when she seeks absolution from the crime of singing before the enemies of the Pope. Her lucidity has the strange effect of underlining her abnormality. It is clear that she cannot help herself. Everything must be subordinated to her singing. The last part of her story functions as a sort of epilogue in which her madness becomes complete, while Ulisse Cavazzaro hangs himself.

In spite of a felicitous selection of episodes, Branzilla's life would lack substance if it were not embedded in a historical context. The opening scene, vaguely reminiscent of Bibi's meeting with the old princess in Thomas Mann's "Das Wunderkind," describes men carrying lorgnettes and wearing black silk clothes. One is transported into the past. Gradually the century is identified. One witnesses the Revolution of 1848, the struggle for Italy's unification, and finally the opening of the gates of Rome to Victor Emmanuel in the year that saw the premiere of *Aïda*. But all events are viewed through Branzilla's eyes; the turmoils of the era parallel, and have a bearing on, her struggle. This makes history an integral part of the tale.

Branzilla herself has little awareness of time. She remembers 'forty-seven as "her year." But basically she denies the passage of time: "Who says that we are old! You, sure, you are old! . . . I am still Branzilla." Thus begins the seventh chapter. The refusal to acknowledge her age is tantamount to a refusal to face her true self. But the author shows us how in the course of the years her deeds have inscribed themselves in her features. As a young, ambitious, but innocent girl, Branzilla meets the world, "the clear lines of her bird profile turned towards the crowd." But old Branzilla stares after her blind husband "bony and rigid with the eyes of a vulture." A kleig light is thrown on the horrors of an egomania which vainly seeks its own guilt in others.

The transformation of the bird profile into the physiognomy of a vulture is of course felt to be gradual. Throughout the tale Mann furnishes traits and gestures which justify the bold terms in which the metamorphosis is stated. Young Branzilla possesses a "hard and sad look." Rupa's invitation is received with "cold submissiveness" accompanied by "small, hard strokes of the fan." As she denies herself all pleasure, Branzilla naturally eats most frugally: "A raw egg, a fennel tea, and that is enough. No wine." Moreover she expects others to discipline themselves just as she does. About her seamstress she says, "She should have made a dress. A perfect dress would have justified her stupid little existence. What does she do instead? She eats, drinks, makes love, and seeks diversions, until there is nothing left of her." And so it is no wonder that men do not visit her dressing room, her "unpleasant mien" perhaps causing her loneliness more than her "angular limbs." But much worse than her furious pursuit of excellence, and much more repelling than her forbidding looks, is her inhuman pleasure in brutally obtained victories. After the death of Amati, Branzilla triumphantly exclaims: "I am not afraid, Signor Sturbanotte. Look how I open and close her eyes. With these lids she will no longer summon any love!" From here to the eyes of a vulture is but a small step.

Unnatural though she is, Branzilla suffers; not as the girl who fights her way to the top, but as the mature singer who senses the dubiousness of her success. It is especially through Cavazzaro that she realizes art is a vampire draining her strength. Art undermines her health while he, the sybarite, grows as a performer. "I must see with my own eyes," she says, "that he has life, and art in addition to it—that very art to which I sacrifice myself; that he plays where I torture myself, and that he nevertheless achieves greatness." She envies her husband and realizes that her attitude toward art is not the only possible one. But she cannot alter her course, and the result is agony.

For the suffering, the conflicts, and the entire abnormality of Branzilla's existence, Mann effectively uses the symbol of darkness. "Die Branzilla" is an "indoor story" in which nature has no place at all. Pathetic fallacy, abundant in "Pippo Spano," is replaced by light and shade. When Branzilla is faced with the decision either to be honest about Rupa's innocence and forgo her debut, or falsely implicate him and sing, her struggle is depicted in the following words:

"He is not my lover. He wanted to hear me sing. Did he love me? I do not love him. What concern of mine is he?" She spoke over her shoulder as if she had to calm someone who might be hidden in the dark; perhaps her aunt Barbara, perhaps something else, something nameless. "He helped me escape misery, you say? Others had heard my singing and yet left me in it?—But did I ask for his help? Did I promise him thanks?"

. . . .

Whenever a new question came from the back, she swiftly turned toward the captain, and in his eyes, which she clearly could see in the shadows, the answer was already decided . . . "Captain, I shall confess."

In this passage darkness is a manifestation of inner turmoil, but also the seat of her conscience. Elsewhere it is a refuge where Branzilla can muster her resources to fight the antagonism of the populace. Rupa's friends having ruined the first act of her debut, she stands, "her forehead against a dark flat on the stage." In the next act she vanquishes their hatred. At times darkness envelops a specific somber thought. "The darkness of the grave" prevails when Branzilla contemplates murdering her husband. But always darkness symbolizes the state of Branzilla's soul when she is not behind the footlights, the splendor of which elates her as a drug does the addict. In darkness she builds her "palace of sounds."

The footlights are the reward for life in the blackness. Thinking about them makes all torture endurable. Yet they are artifices, *lights*, not *light*. Only once does true light come to Branzilla. Cavazzaro, after declaring his love for her, is witness to the violent emotions raging within the breast of his beloved; supreme egotism fights and briefly succumbs to the desire not to be alone: "With frank and open eyes he saw how she, angry and controlled by fear, worked out her struggle. All at once, seized by amazement, he spread his arms. For a glow from within conquered all hardness in her face, all torture, and transformed her. Branzilla became beautiful. All of heaven in her voice, she said, 'I love you!'" Inner radiance lends beauty which man-made illumination cannot produce.

From some of the aspects of "Die Branzilla" discussed thus far, it may have been gathered that the story is written with great economy. The omission of any psychoanalytical remarks concerning the heroine and the absence of any reference to nature accounts in large measure for its amazing brevity. Mann needs less than 11,000 words to bring to life a full half century of an artist's struggle, mistakes, and sorrows. But there are two further techniques that conspire in favor of great concentration. They are

Mann's metonymies and his uncommonly adroit use of the monologue.

On the first page of the story the difference between Branzilla
and a young woman without artistic gifts is expressed as follows:
Branzilla's pale fingertips hold on to a wide skirt "which in a circle
was crushed on the ground." The most desirable girl of Rome, on
the other hand, a member of her first small audience, exuberantly
embraces the singer, and "the embroidered wreaths of her hem
swayed above her little shoes." The carefully observed hems
stand, of course, for the two characters. The Roman socialite is in
harmony with herself and with reality. Branzilla, on the other
hand, appears aggressive and at odds with the world. But the
image points also to her eventual fate, for the ground does not
yield. It is her skirt that is being crushed.

Portions of one monologue have already been quoted. A second
one, taken from the beginning of the second chapter, should
suffice to corroborate the impression of the first and to demonstrate Heinrich Mann's ability to say much in a few words.

. . . . Why are you coming back alone, running and yelling? And
now they even shoot inside the house; are those shots resounding?
And steps in confusion, and wild voices. Tell them that I want to
sing . . . Hurry up!—that I want to sing . . .

What? They are making a Revolution? They are putting His Holiness
to flight? Why, that is impossible! Say that it isn't true! You are afraid,
and you love gossip, old woman, you. They are shooting. What can
it be? Probably just some kind of murder.

No matter; let them shoot; at the theater they will not dare. There
the soldiers of the Holy Father will see to it that I can sing . . . To
be sure, this morning two combs fell from my hair and formed a cross
on the ground . . . And you? You met a hunchback and yet you did
not spit? Because you had your mouth full of candy? And tonight I
am supposed to sing! May that hunchback send all of hell after you!
After you, not me! I must sing!

Confusion, conceit, impatience, peremptoriness, incredulity,
anger, disgust, bravado, superstitiousness, and fiercest determina-
tion are all present in this speech. Added to the belief in bad
omens is the scorn of the ascetic for the aunt's sweet tooth. The

events are told in terms of Branzilla's reaction to them; but it is always clear what is event and what is reaction, what is past and what is present, what is whispered and what shouted. The logic of association is fully transparent. Every aspect of language is exploited: punctuation has the greatest importance for the understanding of the passage; in the German text sibilants set the tone. Simple statements and questions dominate, the only subordinate conjunction being "that"; and the frequent repetition of the word "sing" leaves no doubt about Branzilla's one and only concern.

This type of monologue constitutes about one third of the entire novella. Its theme is always defiance, but there is nothing tedious about its return, since it is never heard twice in the same configuration. The reason for this appears to be that Mann borrows the key and the rhythm of his variations from both the situation and the person or persons to whom Branzilla addresses her words. To the monologue as much as to the entire story apply Bertaux's words about Mann's novelistic art. "Heinrich Mann has evolved a style which has the thrust of dramatic writing but is at the same time not too thin; loaded when circumstances demand it, and yet direct and spare when expressing the rhythm of a bare, hard existence." [28]

The quotation from Bertaux is significant because it makes clear that in spite of all intensifications, "Die Branzilla" is anchored in realism; one might say, even more so than "Der Tyrann." But both tales are in a sense no more than finely executed sketches preliminary to the intricate canvas of *Die kleine Stadt.*

Die kleine Stadt, written between 1907 and 1909, is more than a political novel. Not only did Mann demonstrate here the workings of democracy in the microcosm of an Italian town; he also established relationships between leaders, masses, and individuals in areas other than political, and he furnished a more comprehensive and balanced view of art than ever before. Ulrich Weisstein, discussing briefly and concisely the welding of these three aspects of the novel, called his first article about it *"Die kleine Stadt:* Art, Life and Politics in Heinrich Mann's Novel," [29] "life" being the sum of preoccupations of a citizenry, their businesses, loves, successes, and defeats, their memories and their hopes.

The author's own references to the work under consideration, scattered over many years, tell us what he set out to do, or believed to have done, in it. "My *Little Town* I built for the people, for humanity," he wrote in 1910, and in the following year he declared his hero to be "a community of average men," while once more extolling the naïve sensuality of the Italians, whom he found ideally suited for his literary purposes.[30] Also in 1910, he explained, in an open letter to a critic, how he wanted the political elements understood. "My difficulty was," he said, "that I had to compress a century-long process into a few days. The lowest form of humanity had to clash with its highest (as perhaps really happened in 1791 and 1792), that is to say, in every individual in the crowd, in the crowd itself, and in its leaders." [31] And finally, as regards art, two statements of a much later date show how life and politics came to be transfigured through music:

They [a traveling opera troupe] entered; they moved about; they did things, and had turned the town upside down, when they finally left. The town did nothing but sing. Or, at least, the author, who had the good fortune of living there just then, knew it only singing . . . . He experienced it entirely in choruses and solo parts, without gravity, like music, and the whole life of the little town became one great and beautiful opera performance—much struggle and grief, and even more harmony. It touched him, because he was just prepared inwardly, and because it was exactly the right time for him to write his novel, *Die kleine Stadt*.[32]

And complementary to this:

Be it noted that I always felt him [Puccini] to be the originator not only of passionate song but also of the heightened feeling of his age. It has consequences to make a "little town" sing: in my novel it is the conductor Enrico Dorlenghi who does it. Maestro Puccini did it for a world before all song vanished from it. My young conductor, his burning desire to invent music for a whole nation, is my conception of Puccini developing: I should not have written my novel otherwise.[33]

A miniature French revolution occurring in a small Italian town, brought about by, and eventually dissolved in, music, that is what Heinrich Mann had in mind when he wrote his one-volume "Comédie humaine."

The intricacies of *Die kleine Stadt* make it impossible to summarize the plot in such a way that a background is furnished for a discussion of all of its facets. Therefore, the barest outline is given here, only the central portion of the narrative being presented more fully. A few lengthy quotations set into proper context will, it is hoped, adequately complete the introduction to a work that deserves a monograph of its own.

For the first time in fifty years, an opera troupe visits a drowsy little Italian town.[34] Its arrival brings life into the sleepy community. The troupe's strange unbourgeois element has a fermenting effect, releasing with suddenness the drives and passions of whose existence the provincial hearts had hardly been aware. Quarrels and fights are the result. For extraneous reasons disgruntled citizens strengthen the clerical party of the priest Don Taddeo and help him oppose the progressive forces of the lawyer Ferruccio Belotti. Conservatives watch the struggle with a mixture of glee and indifference, while the one fascist gains a brief moment of glory. Civil war ensues. A fire laid to an inn by an arsonist brings out the fundamental goodness in people while, at the same time, almost destroying Belotti, who is held responsible for the conflagration. But in the end the town's sense of humor and sense of fair play win out. By the time the singers leave, order is restored and everyone except the fascist and his accomplice resumes his place in it. The new harmony resembles the old, with the addition of self-knowledge. Learning what is latent in us and yet affirming reason and humanity, that is what we call progress.

The singers who bring about the temporary upheaval are few, but they are so different from one another that they significantly alter the opinions which one has formed with regard to Mann's view of art and artists from his earlier writings. To be sure, the decadent artist, totally surrendering to art at the expense of life, is still present. It is the prima donna, Flora Galinda, in whom La Branzilla and Mario Malvolto celebrate their resurrection. But others have come with her. Italia Molesin is the lusty type, good-natured, ready to accept lovers indiscriminately, healthy, simple, and somewhat naïve. The Cavaliere Giordano is the aging artist who lives on his past fame and refuses to accept the facts of life. Superannuated and yet unwilling to leave the glamour of the footlights, he would become ridiculous in his vanity, were not his fate almost a tragic one. The futility of his dreams is brought out through the town's old fool, Babrà, who gurgles insinuations to the effect that he, too, once was a great singer. But Giordano makes quick adjustments which allow him to remain in the world of illusion. He is helped by a respectful, understanding society that rewards his past achievements with a memorial plaque.

Nello Gennari reminds one of Branzilla's husband Ulisse Cavazzaro who "has life, and art in addition to it." (VIII, 365) Nello finds his true love in the little town and sings all the better for it. Performance, to him, is an outlet, not an obsession. When he dies by the hand of his beloved—the roles of Othello and Desdemona being reversed—old Barbrà smiles and, with his finger on his lips, urges silence for the two sleepers. And, finally, Virginio Gaddi must be mentioned. A family man and reliable friend of equable character, Gaddi is also a competent baritone, and—for fifty lire extra—a capable stage director. The townspeople appreciate the bourgeois virtues in the artist-craftsman, and when the troupe leaves, they urge him to stay as one of them. "Gaddi!" exclaims the lawyer Belotti, "you who last night [during the fire] exceeded all of us in civic virtue, do you really want to leave us?" And he promises him a good office job. Gaddi recognizes the attractiveness of the offer, but he is an artist at heart. "Would one," he replies, "then as now, however mediocre one's talent as a singer, sometimes feel the great things that life has to give?" And so he declines. The house of art has many mansions; Gaddi's is not the least of them.

Singers are performers. Heinrich Mann rounds out his new comprehensive view of art through the introduction of the conductor and composer Dorlenghi, whose importance has already been pointed out. The creative artist, Dorlenghi, egotistical and conscious of his own merits, is no more removed from the people than is Gaddi. Rather than feeling isolated, he regards art and life to be complementary. "Ambition and the urge to bring happiness, fame and love, are one," says he, and therewith parallels Belotti's pronouncement about the role of the politician: "The ambition of individuals is demanded by the public welfare. Did you ever see a statesman grow in stature without his country's also becoming great?" According to Heinrich Mann's view at the time of writing *Die kleine Stadt,* art, then, is essentially exoteric. It serves a social purpose and gains its strength from being part of life. It demands tolerance; in turn it gives pleasure, insight, and a heightened awareness of one's existence.

Die kleine Stadt is divided into five chapters, the third of which constitutes the apex of a pyramidically constructed novel. It deals with the performance of the opera, "Poor Tonietta," by the fictitious Maestro Viviani.[35] In its hundred pages, Mann reaches his greatest skill in intertwining art and life, making gestures eloquent, and endowing his scene with a *"Vie Unanime."* Structurally this chapter also parallels the novel as a whole. It begins with the effort of the clerical group to interfere with the opera performance; then leads to the hour of expectation within the theater, and reaches a climax with the first act. The intermission marks the beginning of the decline, and a postlude describes the aftermath, until the whole town has gone to sleep. It is, therefore, possible to find in the central hundred pages of the novel not only fine examples of Mann's style, but also salient moments of action which punctuate the preceding and following events.

While the sexton Pipistrelli rings the church bells, his wife and a few other women express their indignation about the devilish work going on in the playhouse. Some craftsmen who are dependent on the church for their livelihood also are there. In vain they try to dissuade passers-by from going to the opera. Don Taddeo, in the meantime, runs after young boys to prevent them from attending the opera, but his zeal is no match for their agility. Belotti appears and demands silence in the name of the people. At this point, Belotti and the priest do not know that they will meet later in more serious challenges; that they will alternately triumph over one another; that in the end they will learn to appreciate each other's virtues. But the basis for all subsequent developments is given in the ringing of the bells and the imperious demand for silence.

The lawyer and his friend, the pharmacist Aquistapace, are seen going to the theater. En route, the jolly lawyer tells of his numerous love affairs, those consummated and those envisaged. As they work their way to their seats, an expectant crowd animatedly discusses private and public matters. Everyone comments on everyone else. But it is the performance of "Poor Tonietta" itself, starting an hour late, that reveals art as a mirror of life. The spectators watch the stage, see themselves, are stimulated to reveal their innermost secrets, and suddenly know who they really are.

The gallery held its breath. Then it began to whisper. "What do they want? . . . They want wine. Those two in front of the house have just been wed, and the others are escorting them home. . . . They sing like the girls in Pozzo when the grapes are being gathered. Do we need actors for that? But they do it better.

. . . .

"And that one looks like Italia," remarked Malandrini, the innkeeper, in his box. "Now she is egging on those boys against the newly-wed couple, saying that Tonietta has deceived her Piero. For that matter she herself deceived the Baron with the lawyer and the rest."

"Hold your tongue!" says his wife, pressing her chin onto her collar and turning red as a turkey cock. "Hold your tongue! You don't know what you are talking about. A man like the Baron is not interested in such—"

She bit her lips. (153 ff.)

It is their own lives which they are watching on stage, but "better." Therefore, fiction and reality cannot be kept apart. Italia is both the character she plays and the one she is off-stage, and Mrs. Malandrini might well bite her lips, for the Baron is also her lover. They are discovered when Don Taddeo, tormented by the vision of Italia in nude embrace, sets fire to the Malandrini inn.

Other moments bring other commentaries and other revelations. After Nello's aria, the applause is great.

"Bis! Bis!"
"Will you be quiet!" hissed Signora Camuzzi to her husband over her shoulder.
"But he sang very well, my dear," said the municipal secretary. "The whole audience thinks so."
"I do not," and she bit her lip. "He is happy," she thought, "but I will have my revenge."
He appeared from the wings, smiling faintly.
"Bis! Bis!"
Signora Camuzzi turned round graciously to her husband.
"You are too good-natured, my friend. Your character may be such

as to make a wife happy, but in public life you should be more ruthless. Why did you agree to lawyer Belotti's proposal to send for these
third-rate actors? Or, if you were unable to prevent it, you ought at
least to have insisted on supervising all the arrangements."

"Do you think so, my dear? The truth is that I did not believe it
would succeed. I was certain that the lawyer would make a fool of
himself. . . . Is your fan broken? I heard it crack." (156 f.)

Madame Camuzzi has once enjoyed Nello's company, but he
never returned, since he fell in love with young Alba Nardini in
the meantime. Her biting her lips signifies the anger of a woman
scorned (whereas Signora Malandrini bites hers from embarrass-
ment). The wife of the municipal secretary is bored and ambitious. She will not be denied. Needling her husband will yield
nothing, as she knows. And so, with the help of one Savezzo, she
will find her revenge by sowing the seeds of suspicion in Alba
Nardini's heart. And when Alba kills Nello and herself, we will
remember the cracking of the fan.

Reference has been made to the town fascist, whose machinations in the field of politics fortunately fail in the end. He, too, is
unmasked by the drama on the stage.

Young Savezzo squinted down his nose at the Club box.

"What do I care about other people's affairs and whether the people
before or behind the curtain live or die. But this concerns only myself,
for only I have a destiny and will triumph over those who hold me
down and become mighty and famous . . . . I might have composed
this music; they have robbed me of that, too." (200)

One can readily imagine by what dishonesty and deviousness this
paranoid character will try to control the town when, during its
great crisis, it remains momentarily without a leader.

In addition to this interplay between the stage and the spectators, there rises above the many individual thoughts, dreams, and
confessions, a group spirit, a collective consciousness, similar to
that in Jules Romain's *Les Copains* or in the agricultural fair of
Madame Bovary. Statements from the crowd, unidentified, belonging to one and to all, mingle with those by individually delineated figures. "A whole people are embracing one another in an
ecstasy of brotherly love," says the old writer Ortensi (162) and

after the performance Dorlenghi exclaims; "So I have seen a people! The people for whom Maestro Viviani wrote his opera. I knew it; we are not alone; a people hears us! . . . In the music of "Poor Tonietta" they recognize their own cadences, their gestures, their rhythms . . . (209).

Dorlenghi's hymn to the unity of art and life is already part of the epilogue. The play is over and people drift home spinning intrigues and rendering account to themselves of what the evening has meant to them. The chapter ends with Nello and Alba sinking into each other's arms, very much in the way they are destined to die later when the *Stagione* of the traveling players in the little town comes to an end.

The passages quoted do not fully reveal Mann's sovereign handling of his material. The predominance of direct discourse which gives the novel its dramatic quality is sufficiently evident, to be sure. But the author also uses other devices to tighten his tale. Often *verba dicendi* are omitted, or replaced by verbs expressing gestures. Instead of simply saying something, the characters whisper, shout, snort, or bluster. Almost every verb simultaneously describes motion and emotion. Speech becomes action; action becomes utterance; and the need for adjectives is greatly reduced. Plain description is also made superfluous by a sort of camera technique. For instance, people listening to an anecdote which they have often heard turn their eyes to the street, observe unimportant events, and then become involved in the anecdote again. Fatigue and lack of attention are converted into an activity. And, finally, there is Mann's skillful introduction, removal, and reintroduction of characters; the disruption of scenes which are continued, quite naturally, in another context; and the echoing of events, seemingly unrelated, and yet reinforcing and elucidating each other.

The overall effect is quite an amazing one. There is probably no other novel of equal density in German literature, no other work that intensifies its realism to a point where cause and effect are absorbed by an explosive vitality and an ordinary tale lingers in one's mind as sheer pulsating life; no other work which allows so clearly a view below the surface of human behavior while depicting the surface only. No wonder that both Heinrich and Thomas Mann regarded it as "Heinrich's best." [36]

CHAPTER 4

The Voice in the Wilderness

I *Activist Essays*

DIE kleine Stadt made it clear that in 1909 Heinrich Mann's "turn toward democracy"[1] was an accomplished fact. He had found the Renaissance ideal wanting. Ruthless individualism did not raise one's *Lebensgefühl.* Democracy, on the other hand, promised to bring vitality to the brotherhood of men. Germany lacked the "sense for public life" which France and Italy possessed. It was time to work in behalf of national democracy and to challenge the forces of anti-intellectualism in one's own country. In 1910 Mann became a moralist, a political thinker, and an author of *littérature engagée.*

He set down his ideas and his program in an essay called "Geist und Tat."[2] Comparing Germany and France, he found that French writers had always been better off than their confreres on the other side of the Rhine. "They had an easy time of it, the writers of France, who, from Rousseau to Zola, opposed existing powers: they had the people." In Germany, the men of the mind had no link with the people. They were not concerned with human dignity. They reflected; they pursued their ideas to the point of the absurd; and they ended in nihilism. By so doing, each of them had been working in behalf of "the sophist justification of injustice, of his deadly enemy: power."

Severing himself completely from the influence of Nietzsche, whom he now regarded as the spiritual forebear of all those who disdained democracy without having known it, Mann asserted the spirit to be democratizing *per se.* "An intellectual who kowtows to the ruling caste commits treason against the spirit," he said, paraphrasing Arnold Acton's rhetorical question, "how can people of culture, how can the intellect, submit to power not derived from the intellect?" And for his program he devised a formulation which seemingly—but only seemingly—implied an abdication of the artist: "the genius . . . as the brother of the lowliest reporter."

In a second essay, also of the year 1910, Mann juxtaposes Voltaire and Goethe.[3] Voltaire was a fighter for freedom, whereas Goethe was aloof and therefore no real force in Germany. "Goethe . . . looks down from the eerie heights, where the German geniuses perhaps understand one another, unmoved, onto his unmoved country. His work, the thought of him, his name have changed nothing in Germany; have eliminated no inhumanity; have opened no inch of road toward a better age." Over the years, the wisdom of the Sage of Weimar had degenerated into glib quotations spouted by those who perpetuated the wrong while living in comfortable sloth. Therefore Heinrich Mann, fully recognizing the all-embracing greatness of Goethe, prefers to follow the path of Voltaire, Balzac, and Zola.

The inclusion of Balzac may seem startling here, but Mann explains that "the unveiling of the wide world, the great game of all human inter-relations is naturally egalitarian." His bias already evident in the comparison of Goethe to Voltaire—why not Racine-Goethe?—becomes even clearer through his mentioning Balzac and Zola. It is the bias of the social novelist against the classical preoccupation with "man" while "men" are suffering.

II *The Kaiser's Subject*

Practice soon followed theory. While publishing some very fine novellas, which in subject matter and spirit still belonged to an earlier period in his creative life, Mann prepared the novel which to this day is regarded as an outstanding political satire. The preliminary studies for it had begun in 1906.[4] *Der Untertan* (this is its title) appeared in installments from 1911 until 1914, when the last part of it had to be left unprinted because of the outbreak of the war. The book as a whole could not be published until 1918.[5] When it appeared, castigating a regime and a society which had just ceased to exist, it was an instant success.

The opinions of the first critics were sharply divided. Those with leftist leanings praised it highly; those of a conservative bent called it a heartless distortion. But they all seemed to agree on one point, namely that *Der Untertan* was first and foremost a well-written political tract and only secondarily a work of literature. With the passage of time, the reactions became less violent, and later interpreters, implicitly or explicitly, acknowledged its artistic merits, without however ranking it as part of the canon of twentieth century German literature. To this day most of those who have occasion to refer to it are cautious not to appear too enthusiastic over a work written with so much acerbity as this one is.

Der Untertan is concerned with the life of one Diederich Hessling—the name echoes the German words for hatred and ugliness—from his childhood to the "height" of his success as a paper manufacturer and patriot. "Diederich Hessling was a sensitive child who liked best to dream, was frightened of everything, and suffered a lot with his ears." This is the opening sentence of the novel. In the second paragraph a sentence begins, "When he had stolen sweets, or when he had lied . . . ," and from then on one follows the young dreamer with *Gemüt*, as he turns his weakness, his fears, and his dishonesties into assets by adapting himself cleverly to the hypocritical society in which he grows up. Individuality is scorned; Diederich scorns individuality. Sexual morality condones the double standard; Diederich ruthlessly exploits the double standard. The bourgeois has to kowtow to the nobility; Diederich kowtows, and passes on the humiliations received from above to those beneath him. The German ideal is the Kaiser; Diederich comes to look and speak like the Kaiser. Faceless himself, he develops into a living mirror of his environment.

His environment is, of course, not entirely made up of people of his ilk. But those who differ in attitude from the vast majority, like the Göppels and the Bucks—Old Man Buck had been a fighter in the Revolution of 1848—are gradually crushed. And so Hessling rises, together with all the other Hesslings, be they governors, district attorneys, or schoolteachers, to ever greater glory through total corruption. His progress accurately measures the moral decline of imperial Germany and foreshadows even the physical ruin of a country which uses fist-shaking and saber-rattling as a means to silence criticism.

The hollowness of Diederich's success is neatly summarized in the fine essay on Heinrich Mann by W. E. Yuill, who is an unqualified admirer of *Der Untertan*.

And so Hessling, assisted and exploited by the aristocracy, arrives at the climax of his career—the unveiling ceremony of a statue to Wilhelm I which has been erected at his instigation. With superb irony Mann puts into his mouth a fiery indictment of the French Second Empire that exactly describes the German Reich:

> "The vital nerve of public life was a mania for advertisement, and again and again it turned into a mania for persecution. Outwardly bolstered up by prestige, inwardly by the police, without any faith other than force, they sought only theatrical effect, made great play with the heroic past, and the only height they scaled was the height of Jingoism."

As Diederich arrives at his peroration, a tremendous thunderstorm breaks, the illustrious company scatters in all directions, and instead of being ceremonially invested, Hessling has a decoration thrust into his hand by a soaking policeman with the words, " 'Ere's yer Order o' William." [6]

Mr. Yuill pays due respect to Mann's political acumen while also transmitting the idea that *Der Untertan* is a very good piece of writing. But he does not analyze the novel with regard to its place in the German literary tradition. This is why Mann's complaint of 1948 is still valid. At that time Mann reported, "A reader of the 'Untertan' wrote to the Aufbau Publishing House that this was no novel but an editorial. . . . Once pigeon-holed by the public as a 'political' novelist, one's formal qualities most of the time remained unnoticed. . . . I should not like to live on as the author of a novelistic editorial." [7] In the following an attempt will be made to do greater justice to Mann's satire by approaching it as an inverted *Bildungsroman*.

The essay "Voltaire-Goethe" may have led people to believe that Heinrich Mann was neither truly familiar with, nor appreciative of, Germany's greatest poet. The contrary is true. And although *Wilhelm Meister* is not expressly mentioned in *Der Untertan*, the story of Diederich Hessling appears to be a parody of it. Just as Adrian Leverkühn's *Dr. Fausti Wehe-klag* in Thomas Mann's *Dr. Faustus* retracts Beethoven's Ninth Symphony, Hessling's life negates the ideal which Wilhelm Meister strives to attain.

Goethe's hero says, "To cultivate myself quite as I am was darkly my wish and my intention from childhood on." He has an "inner need to develop more and more the talent for the good and the beautiful." Erich Truntz, quoting these basic statements adds, " 'Bildung' is shaping through absorption; the question is what becomes fruitful in this process." [8] He then lists the influences which determine Wilhelm's growth: family, love, a circle of men, his child, the theater, pietism, and the nobility. Naturally one cannot expect Heinrich Mann's hero to undergo exactly the same experiences as an eighteenth century character, but insofar as he does, the transmuted parallels are striking.

Diederich Hessling, too, cultivates his native characteristics; only they are the opposite of those which Wilhelm Meister possesses. Diederich is weak, pliable, and selfish. In his cowardly lying and cheating, he is the son of his mother. Even as a boy he evinces a strong anti-intellectualism, distrusting people who express themselves articulately. And above all, he abhors individuality. Void of any sort of self-respect he seeks refuge in groups which strengthen his masochism and its correlative, his sadism.[9]

Diederich was so constituted that he was delighted to belong to an impersonal entity, to this immovable, inhumanly indifferent, mechanical organization which was the college. He was proud of this power, this grim power, which he felt, if only through suffering. On the headmaster's birthday, flowers were placed on the desk and blackboard. Diederich actually decorated the cane. (9)

. . . .

Only once did it happen, when he was in the Lower Third form, that Diederich forgot all prudence, acted blindly and became himself an oppressor, drunk with victory. As was the usual and approved custom, he had bullied the only Jew in his class, but then he proceeded to an unfamiliar manifestation. Out of the blocks which were used for drawing, he built a cross on the desk and forced the Jew onto his knees before it. He held him tight, in spite of his resistance; he was strong! What made Diederich strong was the applause of the bystanders, the crowd whose arms helped him, the overwhelming majority within the building and in the world outside. He was acting on behalf of the whole Christian community of Netzig. How splendid it was to share responsibility, and to feel the sensation of collective consciousness. (11)

This is the boy who must face life and make choices. And German society under William II sees to it that he makes the wrong ones. Kindness, sincerity, and decency sometimes tempt him, but they never really lead him astray. For the persons who offer the alternative to evil always lose out in the struggle with their environment. And for Diederich there exists no other way of evaluating human behavior than success.

Pietism or, for that matter, religion, plays no role in Diederich's development. But the other factors influencing Wilhelm Meister have parallels in the life of Mann's protagonist. Mr. Yuill's brief sketch can bring this out only in part. As do most writers, Yuill also presents Diederich as a rigidly fixed character who merely unfolds. Yet Diederich develops. He begins as a child with a certain potential and ends as Mann's incarnation of the devil. It is worth studying how this comes about.

Diederich's father is an honest, hard-working man and owner of a small paper mill. All his attitudes reveal the non-commissioned officer of three Bismarckian wars. His mother, on the other hand, is sentimental, lazy, and devious. The son stands in awe of his father but he loves his mother; loves her sincerely while at the same time disdaining her. It is she who "spoils him for life."

Love comes to Diederich while he is studying chemistry in Berlin. Agnes Göppel, the daughter of a business friend of father Hessling, bestows her affection upon him. She is so womanly, so natural and direct, that she embarrasses him, as decency always does. He, nevertheless, is attracted to her. She becomes his mistress, secretly hoping for eventual marriage, but she is careful never to make any demands on him. Her independence both intrigues and disturbs him. Had she been wealthy, he might have married her. But since Mr. Göppel's affairs are not in the best order, he eventually frees himself from her, later rejecting her father's pleas in behalf of his unhappy daughter with the words, "my moral sense forbids me to marry a girl who does not bring her maidenly purity as her marriage portion."

The circle of men which exercises the strongest influence on Diederich is his fraternity. The members of the Neo-Teutons drink and sing; this is their sole reason for meeting. They sing of freedom and they drink because the beer "transformed itself into inner freedom." (29) In their midst Diederich experiences the intoxication of being nothing. The abrogation of any personal dignity is cultivated here and prepares the students for life in a cone-shaped society. "Each one of us is as nothing, but massed in ranks as Neo-Teutons, soldiers, bureaucrats, priests and scientists, as economic organizations and unions of power, we taper up like a pyramid to the point at the top where power itself stands, graven and dazzling." (58/45) When Diederich obtains his degree and leaves his drinking companions, his apprenticeship as a loyal subject to his monarch is over. He knows how to act as a part of a group; and he knows how to bow to those above him while trampling on those below him.

The theater enters into Diederich's development in several ways. Most importantly, all of public life under William II is understood to be one gigantic piece of play-acting. The Kaiser's way of ruling is nothing but the boastful gesture of an "alleged personality." The fiction of lord and loyal subject gives German life "the air of wretched mummery." (227/177) This is why Wolfgang Buck, Diederich's sensible contemporary, leaves the stage and returns to practising law. Where everyone play-acts, there is no purpose in representing, in front of an audience of unauthentic characters, "lofty morality, the intellect and the soul of modern man." (437/301)

But as one may expect in a Heinrich Mann novel, actual performances are also described. The eight pages devoted to Hessling's attending and interpreting *Lohengrin* have elicited encomiums even from critics who heartily disliked the rest of *Der Untertan*.[10] A vignette of devastating humor, it was omitted from the English translation. This is regrettable for, in the hands of Heinrich Mann, Wagner's music drama becomes the perfect image of the *Kaiserreich*, an image of the tritest chauvinistic bombast.

Another scene involving the theater is less well-known but equally significant. It is that of an amateur performance at the Harmony Club. Countess Wulckow, the wife of the district governor, has written a play in which a young Countess is driven by her cousin to marry a music teacher, which makes her ineligible to share in her uncle's estate. Marrying beneath her station, she also loses the privilege of attending royal receptions. This sad fate, however, harmonizes with a higher will that demands large fortunes to remain intact. The local citizenry of the small town of Netzig feels obliged and honored to act out and applaud Frau von Wulckow's wretched melodrama. The brainwashing functions of the play are obvious, but Heinrich Mann deepens his criticism by revealing it to be nothing but a travesty of Goethe's *Natürliche Tochter* (*Natural Daughter*). A Junker's wife has turned the spirit of Weimar into the defense of a mendacious system.

Having made his monarch's histrionics his own, having acquired the ability to act only as the member of a group, having found ways to calm his conscience whenever an honest individual makes him feel uneasy, and having accepted his middle class status, Diederich Hessling has to learn only one other thing, namely, how to conceal his corruptness. This he is taught by the nobility, and especially by Governor von Wulckow. Wulckow wants Hessling's property at a bargain price for his cousin von Quitzin. Diederich offers Wulckow a bribe in the form of some other real estate which can be sold at a profit to the town of Netzig. The wrath of righteous indignation descends on poor Diederich. "A damned tradesman has the cheek to presume that the representative of His Majesty the King will take a hand in dirty deals!" thunders von Wulckow, and Diederich apologizes. But soon thereafter he is pressured into selling to von Quitzin through a third party, the Governor staying officially out of the shady transaction. The lesson Diederich learns is so expensive that he never forgets it. Now Diederich's education is complete. He enters politics and becomes a city councilman. His rhetoric more and more resembles that of the Kaiser, and his machinations those of the Junkers. He becomes wealthy as the tool of the governing classes. Titles and medals replace honor. And after the unveiling of the statue—the highpoint in his career described by Mr. Yuill—when he appears at the bedside of old Mr. Buck, horror spreads over the face of the dying liberal. "He has seen the devil!"

III   *The Brothers' Quarrel*

In the concentration on Diederich Hessling and his "rake's progress," one is apt to neglect the purely political aspects of *Der Untertan*. Yet they are present and their essence is the "brinkmanship" perpetrated by the emperor and his followers. His Majesty's saber rattling is intended to cover up social decay, but it cannot help doing something far more dangerous at the same time. The Germany of William II and Diederich Hessling, as depicted by Mann, is clearly headed for war.

When the war actually broke out, Heinrich Mann had reasons to be proud of his keenness. But beyond that he had reasons to be struck by the similarity between his own novelistic *oeuvre* and that of Zola. In 1869, Zola had said, "For my work, for the sake of its logic, I need the downfall of these people! No matter how often I think the drama through to its end, the end is always their downfall. As things stand in reality, it is not probable that the end will come soon. But I need it." [11] And within the year, the Franco-Prussian War broke out. The parallel between the two political prophets was too impressive to be ignored. In 1915, Mann wrote his Zola essay.

In this essay, the life of the French novelist is traced from his beginnings as a "poetizing youth" to his death. But the reader soon realizes that much more is to be learned from it about Mann than about Zola. Having noticed his resemblance with the author of the *Rougon Maquart* series in one respect, Mann looks for others, finds several, and, where none are to be discovered, he invents them. This is most conspicuously the case with regard to the Dreyfus affair. Germany had no similar scandal, and so Zola's "j'accuse" is subtly transformed into an attack against those German authors who implicitly or explicitly supported the cause of the German empire before and during the First World War.

One passage in particular, directed quite pointedly at brother Thomas, produced a controversy of some scope. At the beginning of the war, Thomas had written an essay on Frederick the Great, showing his sympathy for the king who, to this day, symbolizes the Prussian spirit. To be sure, he depicted him as a kind of royal Gustav Aschenbach, a "moralist of achievement," fulfilling his manifest destiny with a sense of irony concerning his mission. But no equivocation could remove the praise implicit in the choice of subject matter; nothing could take away the implicit glorification of the Kaiser, who, after all, was also a king of Prussia. Furthermore, the essay furnished, by implication, a justification of Germany's attack on neutral Belgium. In reference to this Heinrich inserted the following remarks into his essay:

Intellectuals are neither amateurs nor craftsmen of the spirit. A person does not become one by practicing certain professions. Still less does he become one through lascivious fondling of phenomena of the mind

[74]

—and least of all do I mean those babblers of profundity who furnish intellectual crutches for the non-intellectual, who imagine that they have insights, and beyond all insights they could be eulogizers of ruthless power.[12]

Thomas replied by writing his *Betrachtungen eines Unpolitischen* (*"Meditations of a Nonpolitical Man"*).[13]

The *Betrachtungen* are a curious defense of Germany's "hate-inspiring 'uniqueness,'" (17) and a protest against the "politicization of the spirit." (xxxiii) Its more than six hundred pages of insight and error, logic and paradox, cool objectivity and acrimonious emotionalism, primarily concern the student of Thomas Mann and his works. But a number of remarks are also of interest to the student of Heinrich; some, because they cast a light on Heinrich's development, others because they later influenced the writings of both men.

First and foremost, Thomas, more than anyone else at the time, recognized that his brother's new role of social critic and political activist did not constitute a real break with his past; that Heinrich, in spite of new themes and objectives, was still the esthete he had always been:

On these pages I seemingly have accepted and appropriated for myself the contrast between political and politicized art, and esthetic art. But that was a game; for deep down I know better how it is with this contrast; I know that it is based on an intentional . . . and only too successful self-deception on the part of him who postulates it; that it is false; that it does not exist; that one need not be an esthete in order not to believe in politics, but that as a "serving" socio-moralist and proclaimer of resolute love for humanity one may have remained an archesthete." (560)

This possibility is a certainty for Thomas as far as his older brother is concerned: "We used to have the hysterical Renaissance —now we have hysterical democracy." (561)

Why did Thomas Mann accept the former but not the latter? Simply because the very expression "hysterical Renaissance," placed by Heinrich in the mouth of Jacobus Halm in *Die Göttinnen*, betrayed the kind of irony and introspection which Thomas liked. The new Heinrich, on the other hand, seemed deadly serious and concerned with practical results. This is contrary to the nature of art, and Heinrich knew it. Therefore Thomas accused his brother of creating brilliant verbal fireworks merely in order to win the applause of the multitude:

In the final analysis, heaven knows, he is an artist, and what validity do opinions have in the realm of art? Fundamentally he knows that they do not count. Who would care to judge an artist by his opinions —or a work of art, even an eloquent one, by its possible consequences . . . the political artist is the artist most hungry for *effect* but he covers up his hunger for effect with the doctrine that art must have consequences and, to be sure, political ones." (563)

For the type of man Heinrich had become in Thomas's eyes, the younger brother then coined a term which denied both Heinrich's art and his patriotism. He called him a *Zivilisationsliterat*—literateur of civilization.

The *Zivilisationsliterat,* Thomas explains, is a man who wishes to Romanize Germany. He represents the Western spirit, that is to say, the French spirit, in contrast to the basic German spirit. The French spirit expresses *ratio* through words—*Zivilisationsliterat* therefore is a pleonasm—whereas the German spirit speaks through music. The former is concerned with social man; the latter, with the inner man. The former acts in behalf of "civilization" in contradistinction to "culture," which the latter seeks to foster.

Vague though Thomas's coinage may be, its two pejorative implications are clear. Zola had been looking forward to the defeat of the third Napoleon. But hoping for a French regeneration from within, he had not been concerned with the *agent* of this defeat. Heinrich Mann, on the other hand, wanted more than a debacle for Germany; while not caring about French nationalism or military victory, he did wish for French intellectual dominance over Germany. Thomas intentionally did not differentiate between the intellectual conquest which Heinrich desired and the military conquest which the latter feared. Secondly, Thomas called his brother a *Literat*. In German, an author of artistic rank is called a *Dichter*, irrespective of the genre he favors. *Literat* smacks of the sub-literary even more than does "literateur" in English. Thomas might have called his brother *Zivilisationsdichter,* or perhaps,

Schriftseller. By not so doing, he retracted all the professions of admiration that can be found throughout the *Betrachtungen.* Thomas's coinage did much harm to Heinrich, since innumerable lesser minds used it for years to dismiss summarily all of the latter's achievements. Only recently has the impact of the Mephistophelian epithet lost its force.[14]

Quite naturally the two brothers ceased to be friends for several years. During this period Heinrich converted the epithet created for him into a name of honor, but significantly enough, he did not apply it to himself, but to an intellectual who was a practical politician, namely Kurt Eisner.[15] When the mutually inflicted wounds healed, Heinrich removed the offensive passage from his Zola essay and Thomas came to see "the quarrel in the house of Mann" in a more objective light, as is evident from *The Magic Mountain.* Erich Heller states it this way:

> This, then, is how the two brothers face each other: the one, nobly enraged by the ignominy of the ruling powers, courageously proclaiming with catastrophic platitudes his belief in a better future; the other, indignant at the untruth of high-minded and high-falutin rhetoric, supporting with many a true insight into the human condition an insupportable cause. It is the exact picture that Thomas Mann himself was later to draw of the struggle, with Naphta and Settembrini fighting it out in The Magic Mountain, paradigmatic victims, perhaps, of one of the most disturbing perversions of an age in which all profundities tend to be sinister, and shallow all the friendlier thoughts about man.[16]

IV *An Ideal*

While Thomas wrote his *Betrachtungen*—they were not published until 1918—Heinrich worked on his second novel concerning the German Empire. It appeared in 1917 under the title, *Die Armen* ("The Poor"). This time the proletariat was the focus of his interest. However, he did not succeed in giving the characters the kind of life and profile which those of *Der Untertan* possess. As a document this book may have its merits; but as a novel it does not.[17] If a first edition is still prized, it is only because it was illustrated by Käthe Kollwitz.

1917 was also the year in which *Madame Legros* had its premiere. This drama, the only one among his stage works which Heinrich Mann took seriously,[18] had been written in 1913. But "it bided its time." [19] Four years later the moment was propitious. "Toward the end of the war," Mann recalls in his memoirs, "the Germans could not be aroused to anger, not in my way; in another, only weakly. . . . But I accomplished this much: that they were taken aback and thought of their better days." [20] He really had accomplished more; he had written a good play which the public and most reviewers liked very much.

Mann found his plot in Michelet's *Histoire de la révolution française*. Its outline is sketched in the Zola essay.

He [Zola] appears now in his feeling as simple as any simple figure of once-upon-a-time who brought about a miracle merely through strength of heart. More than a hundred years earlier a woman had gone through the same Paris, a woman of the lower bourgeoisie; had gone from one person to another, great gentlemen, people in the street, the Queen herself; and to each one, in spite of mockery, fatigue, and danger, she said only one thing, namely that an innocent man was sitting in the Bastille, that the innocent man had to be freed, or else the world could not continue to exist a day longer. She succeeded, too; it seemed strange and stirred souls. But only much later did it become clear that it had been an emotional prelude to the Revolution.[21]

This is an outline of the play rather than of Michelet's account. The real prisoner Latude was not in the Bastille but in Bicêtre. His liberation took place in 1784, not in 1789. And he was not innocent, but a mentally unbalanced character who deserved to be incarcerated, though not perhaps for a whole lifetime.

Mann's Madame Legros is instinctively virtuous. Once she knows of a specific injustice, she cannot but devote herself fully to its rectification. Her path is a tortuous one. She must make people do the right thing for the wrong reasons. She learns that one cannot act without becoming guilty oneself. To free Latude, she has to make a spectacle of herself in the streets and in the salons; she has to betray an Austrian agent; and she has to promise herself to a chevalier. But nothing deters her, and she cannot be sullied for long, since her motives are pure.

Needless to say, she is the dominant character in the drama. The others, including Queen Marie Antoinette, remain shadowy. But the heroine's outer difficulties and inner complexities are such as to make one forget this. Where a whole society is the antagonist, the delineations of secondary figures, whether they represent a class or an age, are not of paramount importance. Furthermore, Mme Legros achieves what Shaw's St. Joan only plans: after Latude is rescued, she humbly returns to her husband's linen shop.[22] M. Legros' readjustment to his wife, who rose to fame and now comes back as if nothing had happened, and Mme Legros' convincing dismissal of her moment of glory keep the play interesting to the end.

Alfred Kerr, the dean of German critics, took exception to the language of *Madame Legros*. "The eighteenth century never spoke that way; it is the speech of an imperfect translation from the eighteenth century." [23] Kerr had a fine ear. Mann's language is a little stiff and stylized. But this is hardly a weakness, for the overall effect is that of understatement and controlled emotion. In retrospect one may see anticipated in the tension between the calm, even stilted words and the pathos behind them, one of the major elements of *Neue Sachlichkeit*. The profound humanity of the play, stated with determined reticence, probably also accounts for the fact that it has been brought to the stage recently again—a fate which Mann's other dramas are not like to share.

CHAPTER 5

The Wilderness in the Voice

I A Sick Republic

THE years between 1918 and 1933 constitute exactly the center of Mann's life as a writer. Eighteen creative years precede them and eighteen more follow them. But the center does not represent a peak. If one looks at the quantity of Mann's production, no slackening of his powers is noticeable. The quality, however, leaves something to be desired. Very few of the five novels, fourteen novellas, three dramatic works, and close to two hundred essays and occasional pieces are still read.

Why should this be so? One answer that comes to mind concerns the ambiguous fame which Mann had achieved by the end of the war. He was renowned as the greatest of those German writers "who make it their task not only to give shape to our century in their books but also to transform it through them." [1] Having seen the disastrous events that took place in Europe, and having prepared the way for the Weimar Republic, he had, of course, an interest in its welfare. When asked to give it direction and to defend it, he readily agreed, delivering many addresses and writing numerous newspaper articles. But since he also was highly reputed as an artist, he was frequently called upon to judge books, to interpret German literary trends for other countries, and to eulogize friends and colleagues on various occasions. All of these duties, which he cheerfully assumed, forced him to scatter his efforts and spread himself thin.

A second reason, however, and one recognized by Mann himself, is equally important. It is this: with the end of the war, the world which Heinrich Mann had analyzed in his work had come to an end as well. It had been an imperfect and mixed-up world, but a stable one. What followed was a period of extreme instability. In 1927 he said, "It seems difficult to me to write a social novel and a real novel today. Too many facts obscure one's vision. The picture of the whole will not take shape until later, when we shall have achieved a greater distance." [2]

Speaking subjectively, he was right, but it must be pointed out here that other authors succeeded where Heinrich Mann failed. During the period under consideration, Thomas Mann's *Zauberberg* (*Magic Mountain*) was written; so were Döblin's *Berlin Alexanderplatz* and Hermann Broch's *Die Schlafwandler* (*The Sleepwalkers*); and Robert Musil's *Der Mann ohne Eigenschaften* (*The Man Without Qualities*), although not completed, was then being composed. Hence an overview was possible, but it demanded more patience than Heinrich Mann possessed, and different stylistic means from those which he had developed. Above all, it demanded knowledge other than the kind which he had at his disposal. His phrase, "a real novel," is telling. He was thinking of the novel as "a mirror on the highway,"—in his Stendhal essay a whole paragraph is built on this Stendhalian expression—believing that society had to furnish the symbols for itself. But society no longer yielded any symbols, at least not to German novelists. Thomas Mann found them in medicine, mythology, and music. Döblin was a physician; Broch a logician; and Musil had a thorough academic training both as an engineer and a psychologist.[3] Small wonder, then, that Heinrich Mann did not compose another first-rate long narrative until he, too, had mastered an ancillary science. It happened to be history. His historical studies, however, did not bear fruit until after he left Germany. During the constantly changing years of the Weimar Republic, his attempts to describe reality yielded few pages of real merit. Between understanding and annoyance, certainty and doubt, hope and despair, Mann floundered.

This is not to say that one can simply dismiss in toto his labors of fifteen years. Someone interested in German literature around 1920 will find many good ideas in Mann's essay dealing with this subject. Students of Wedekind or Anatole France can discover very felicitous formulations in the few pages devoted to them. And political scientists can profit greatly from reading "The Tragedy of 1923," the various remarks concerning Russia, or the pieces dealing with the unification of Europe.

Naturally, much of this, be it ever so well expressed, belongs to the history of civilization. The present study, therefore, must bypass it.[4] But at least two short stories are important, one novel proves still to be very readable, and one essay is outstanding. These will be discussed here in some detail. The lesser novels will be treated somewhat more briefly, but it would not do to ignore them entirely. When a man has achieved the stature of Heinrich Mann, even his failures are of interest.

The first of the two stories to be considered is "Der Gläubiger" ("The Creditor"). It appeared in 1924, chronologically preceding the five novels. In this tale, two contemporaries of Diederich Hessling base their lives on an act of cowardice and on a lie. The lawyer Liban and Emma Blasius would like to get married. But Liban is poor, and Emma's parents reject him as a suitor. The two lovers do not dare to go against the wishes of her parents. "The whole strongly solidified order in those peaceful times favored the parents." The difference between the older and younger generations is the difference between those who grew up under Bismarck and those who grew up under William II. Echos of *Der Untertan* and *Die Jagd nach Liebe* are perceptible here. Both Emma and Liban grudgingly consent to financially more advantageous matches. While Emma's husband, Dr. Schatz, is ill, she and Liban drift into an illicit affair, not knowing that Emma's little boy, Wolf, has observed them. Dr. Schatz dies shortly after the outbreak of the war. Liban, now a judge, handles his affairs and those of his paramour, doing rather well during the war years. But when, after the war, the inflation sets in with full force, he meets with hard times. Just then, Wölfchen leaves the Gymasium and joins the speculators and profiteers. Though hardly of voting age, he proves to be a first-rate *débrouillard* who helps his mother preserve her fortune, while Liban is reduced to his devalued salary. Wölfchen's immorality, by no means limited to black-marketeering, is ingenuous. He regards his overt ruthlessness as superior to the mendacity of his mother and Liban. His monetary success renders him invulnerable to the feeble attempts of Liban to assert his authority. Wolf takes one of Liban's daughters on a trip and Liban is neither financially nor morally able to impose on the children those standards to which he, himself, has paid no more than lip service. In fact, Wolf makes it clear that Liban's other daughter will also travel with him.

The conflict of generations, which plays no role in the literature of the *fin du siècle*, is an important theme in Expressionism. The accusations made by Wölfchen against his elders are the same as those which one can hear in the works of Hasenclever, Toller, or Kaiser, for example. But the introduction of the inflation and the realistic description of the amoral younger generation gives to "Der Gläubiger" a note that is unmistakably Mann's.

From the point of view of style, the tale exhibits Mann's direct and sparse language at its best.[5] The author is most effective in capturing the tone of the spoken word and in condensing a whole personality into a single phrase. One brief scene may serve as an illustration. When Emma reveals to Liban that she is not allowed to marry him, the two face each other. " 'And Dr. Schatz?' he asked. She confessed: 'Papa has explicitly forbidden that I simply drop him.'—'In that case . . . ,' said the young man." In German, Liban's lame reply evokes a gesture of resignation and reveals the weakness of his character more completely than could any lengthy analysis of his state of mind by an omniscient author.

The second novella of interest was published in 1925 under the title "Kobes." The main character of this tale is an influential industrialist modeled after Hugo Stinnes, whom the *Petit Larousse* still lists as one of the perpetrators of the great inflation. This makes "Kobes" unique, for the vast literature about the turbulent post-war years in Germany—all but forgotten with the exception of Thomas Mann's "Disorder and Early Sorrow"—deals largely with the victims of the rapid devaluation of the mark. Another reason that "Kobes" is *sui generis* is its style. Matching the illustrations of George Grosz in explosiveness and monstrous distortion, it is Mann's outstanding contribution to literary expressionism.

Although one needs no historical explanation to experience the impact of the novella, a few remarks on the inflation may prove helpful. During the war the German mark gradually lost its buying power, but in 1918 it still had about 50% of its pre-war value. From 1918 on, the decline of the mark accelerated. In December of 1921 one dollar purchased 190 marks. In December of 1922, one dollar was worth 7,650 marks. During 1923 the fall of the mark took on dizzying speed. In August the dollar was worth 1,100,000 marks, in September, 9,700,000 marks, during the month of October the dollar rose from 242,000,000 to 72,500,000,000 marks. When the mark was stabilized in November, one mark in new hard currency corresponded to 4,200,000,000,000 paper marks.[6] The damage produced by such monetary chaos defies the imagination. Only a few industrialists in the Ruhr district understood the simple principle: buy today and pay tomorrow, through which they accumulated tremendous wealth while governments and the common people went bankrupt. Stinnes was the most prominent among these and therefore lent himself well to Mann's Orwellian tale.

The novella opens with a taut, fast-paced scene in which a burgher runs a wild Marathon race in order to be the first to report that Kobes has been elected. Kobes is always being elected, by everyone and for everything. He is the profiteer on a large scale and the undisputed master of Germany. But the author is not content with recreating in words the atmosphere of madness pervading the inflation, nor merely to depict the man who best understood its nature. Rather, he hyperbolizes, and so conjures an apocalyptic vision. Kobes is Moloch, a myth, a power on whose altar the middle-class unwittingly sacrifices itself.

Kobes is surrounded by innumerable lieutenants of various echelons. His immediate subordinates actually form a cabinet. They do his work and keep the populace away from him. Their aims are total: "'Dismantling of the social system!' [says the chief of Propaganda].—'Reduction of salaries,' interjected the section chief for Savings. 'Reduction of the Civil Service.'—'Reduction of cultural life!' demanded the section chief for Cultural Matters. 'Reduction of life,' concluded the section chief for Social Affairs." They cultivate the myth of Kobes in the most daring manner. When Kobes speaks on the radio, it is not his own whistling voice one hears, but the mellifluous one of an announcer who drones, "Kobes does not carouse; Kobes does not drink; Kobes does not whore; Kobes works twenty hours a day." The public image created is so mysterious as to make Kobes' very existence questionable. The highest-ranking officers in the Kobes organization tell about their encounters with him without quite believing one another. He does, however, exist. The reader comes to know him as a person who thinks of himself as a dedicated and ascetic businessman, innocently fulfilling his destiny.

Kobes has one hidden opponent. It is an employee of his in

charge of the supervision of cabarets in the Department of Propaganda. This employee has, tritely enough, a small frail body and a large philosopher's head. He sets out to annihilate Kobes by exalting him to the point of absurdity. When Kobes has swallowed up all there is, so the little man thinks, then he must needs be full, defenseless, the prey of his own greed, and ready to be killed.

But the intellect cannot succeed by exaggerating the methods of the anti-intellect. Chance at first helps the little man. He manages to coerce Kobes into making him his chief of propaganda. Then he engages an actor who produces for him a devilish performance designed to deify Kobes and to turn all workers into hypnotized worshipers of the new Kobes religion. The black mass on the stage is a success. The children of the workers gladly jump into a blast furnace. But the keenest and most zealous of Kobes' servants is witness to the spectacle and sees through the little man's game. He is the head of the Social Department, a handsome young man with a shark's mouth. His countermeasures are quick and effective. The actor is kidnaped and may henceforth perform only in insane asylums, so that the Walpurgis Night of big industry staged by him is thoroughly discredited. The small man finds out that he is no match for the "shark's mouth." The latter speaks to him with supercilious pity: "Ignorant child! Is a blast furnace refuted when one jumps into it? Is Kobes dead, if you make stupid jokes about him? . . . You don't know any joke that can kill the system." Reduced through treachery from chief of propaganda to elevator operator, and aware of his impotence, the small man of intellect kills himself.

Someone born after 1920 who reads "Kobes" now is not likely to think first of the events of 1923, but rather of the period from 1933 to 1945, for in the character of Kobes, Hitler seems to have been anticipated. The inflation fuses in one's mind with the Third Reich. The "shark's mouth" strikingly resembles Goebbels, and it does not take too fanciful an imagination to see other parallels between Kobes' and the Führer's cabinets. "Kobes," besides being a unique kind of story about the inflation, could be a frighteningly good handbook for dictators.

It has been mentioned before that "Kobes" is an expressionistic story. Kantorowicz speaks of "its hectic, expressionistic style which makes every sentence an outcry, which draws people with the utmost terseness and concentration in outline. . . ." [7] Americans know this manner of writing from Kaiser's *From Morn to Midnight*, from Elmer Rice's *Adding Machine*, and from works of Dos Passos. It has never been used with greater justification than in Mann's portrayal of an era of madness.

"Kobes," like "Der Gläubiger" and a few others of Heinrich Mann's works dealing with the immediate post-war years, had the misfortune of appearing during the brief spell of prosperity which providence granted the Weimar Republic. The inflation was no longer news and not yet history. But of late the critics have begun to appreciate the documentary and artistic value of Mann's grotesque comments on grotesque times.

1925 was also the year of *Der Kopf*, the third of the novels depicting pre-World War I Germany. Since its appearance, *Der Untertan, Die Armen* and *Der Kopf* ("The Leaders") have been known as the "Kaiserreich trilogy." "*Der Kopf* is a book of remembrances," Heinrich Mann wrote to Johannes R. Becher, "since I experienced consciously the *Kaiserreich* from the last years of Bismarck on. After the bourgeois (*Untertan*) and the workers (*Die Armen*) I wanted to depict the stratum of intellectuals, their various species, all with reference to the fate of the Reich." [8] The author's purpose necessitated a set of characters completely different from those presented in the two preceding novels. *Der Kopf*, being the novel about the leaders, therefore has little to do with the stories of Diederich Hessling or of the worker Balrich; and the trilogy is not quite a trilogy in the same sense as *Die Göttinnen*.

Mann worked on this 637-page opus for seven years. When he conceived the plan for it, the Empire of William II was in its death throes; when he completed it, the Weimar Republic was at its peak. When he started it, he thought he would have to hide his critique behind fictitious names of persons and places. By 1925 this was no longer necessary. The quickly changing scene demanded constant revisions, and in the course of seven eventful years many new ideas had to be incorporated in the work. This, according to some critics, prevented *Der Kopf* from being of a piece; it kept the characters from being delineated in a consistent manner. To be sure, N. Serebrow begins his article with the sentence "The novel *Der Kopf* (1925) belongs undoubtedly to the most significant works by Heinrich Mann," [9] but his is a lonely voice. No one else has praised the novel recently without strong reservations.

There is not even agreement on its main theme. According to Thomas Mann, the "most accomplished thing" in it is the friendship of two men "whose interlocking destinies are infected with a melancholy of contradictory ideas and of human shortcomings." [10] According to East German scholars, *Der Kopf* is essentially a political novel. The latter interpretation places the emphasis where it belongs, since the fictitious heroes, Mangolf and Terra, are surrounded by thinly disguised historical figures. The chancellors von Bülow and Bethmann-Hollweg appear as Count Lannas and von Tolleben; Admiral von Tirpitz appears as Fischer; "L'Eminence grise," Count Holstein, appears as von Gubitz; and Gerhart Hauptmann appears as Hummel. Furthermore, actual historical events are discussed without camouflage, and Bismarck and the Emperor enter into the novel without pseudonyms. The facts that Terra has some characteristics borrowed from Wedekind and that Wedekind's language is also consciously used in some of Lannas' speeches[11] detract in no way from *Der Kopf* being largely a political *roman à clef*.

Mann's main point seems to be this: in the days of the Empire, Germany lacked proper leadership. The politicians were weak compromisers. German society had no room for true talents. The intellectuals, in so far as they were concerned with politics, were beset by inner conflicts which did not allow their efforts to become effective. A vacuum resulted which was quickly filled by the military and by big industry, whose machinations could lead to nothing but a fiasco.

In the novel, the intellectuals are represented by Mangolf and Terra. Mangolf is guided only by ambition. He therefore joins in the game which is being played by those in power. Terra is a far more complex character than his friend, and much too contradictory to be believable. He works in turn as a barker, a pimp, a spy, a lawyer for the poor, a member of the German Reichstag, and a representative for the armaments industry. Essentially, he is an idealist with a desire for adventure, and totally unsure of the means by which ideals can be made a reality. Lannas characterizes him as follows: "I have lived abroad a long time; I know the type of intellectual champion of life who through all sorts of wild professions and experiences finally either gets into a regular career, as if through providence, or possibly does not, and who characterizes the nature of democracies." (209) As a combination of a Marquis Posa, to whom he actually is likened (314), and Wedekind's Marquis Von Keith,[12] he occasionally tries to improve the political situation, sometimes by leading evil to excess so that its absurdity becomes patent. But being at all times an overwrought character, he fatigues the reader, so that his suicide, committed jointly with Mangolf, no longer interests those few who muster the patience for reading the novel to its end.

The plot consists of intrigues and counter intrigues, of small and large conspiracies boxed into one another, of acts of revenge, and of fantastic tom-fooleries. It is possible that some of the incredible scenes described—reminiscent of the stories that are told about the smoke-filled rooms during the Harding administration in America—have a factual basis. But they lack the kind of verisimilitude needed in a work of fiction, and since they depict confusion from the point of view of confused heroes, they do not linger in one's memory.

To the student of Heinrich Mann, *Der Kopf* is not totally without value. Numerous autobiographical elements are evident in the first part of the novel. Goethe is quoted, echoes of Balzac can be heard throughout, and even Kleist's essay on the Marionette Theater seems to have been in Mann's mind.[13] But nothing really can rescue the work, and it is no accident that it has not been reprinted in German since 1931.[14] Heinrich Mann must have sensed its weakness when he suggested that, in a volume of representative excerpts from his work, *Der Kopf* should only be mentioned by its title.[15]

II *The Perplexed Novelist*

Mutter Marie (*Mother Mary*) followed two years after *Der Kopf*. It is the first of three novels in which the virtues of a sense of duty and optimism are extolled, presumably to balance the pessimism expressed in the three books about the Wilhelminian Empire. All three, not only *Mutter Marie* but also *Die grosse*

Sache ("The Big Deal") and *Ein ernstes Leben* (*The Hill of Lies*), are weak. All three contain elements of the detective story and the sensational novel. But *Mutter Marie* is probably the weakest.

In the center of *Mutter Marie* stands an adventuress who, from humblest beginnings, has risen to a position of titled wealth. As Baroness von Hartmann, she goes in search of her son, whom she had abandoned as an infant and who has grown up in the family of an impecunious former general. When she finds her son again, she devotes her life to him, while simultaneously trying to win him back. She is selfish, but the Catholic faith of her childhood eventually helps her overcome her egotism. After many years she returns to the Church, confesses all her past sins, and gives up her son, in order not to stand in the way of his happiness.

Loosely constructed and in part negligently written, the novel still shows Heinrich Mann's hand. This is particularly evident in the secondary figure of the son, Valentine. He is one of those young men who, returning from the war, cannot find places in the chaos of Germany. The former lieutenant becomes a sort of gigolo and gambler, but one with a good heart and a sense of responsibility. Valentine has numerous brothers in the minor works of Heinrich Mann. Though not a veteran, Wölfchen in "Der Gläubiger" is his brother, and so are the children of Birk in *Die grosse Sache*. Others exist in stories and playlets not discussed in this study.[16] But none of them has been sufficiently realized to become representative of his type—a fact which must be regarded as a sign of Mann's uncertain groping.

Eugenie oder Die Bürgerzeit (trans. as *Royal Woman*) appeared in 1928 and stands quite apart from Heinrich Mann's other works. Professor Weisstein sees in it "a kind of counterpart to *Buddenbrooks*,"[17] though its fairy tale ending might also make one think of *Royal Highness*. But even more closely related to it than Thomas' novels are some of Fontane's works, which Heinrich liked as well as did his brother. Kantorowicz speaks of the "soft pastel shades" which set off *Eugenie* from the satires drawn "with powerful strokes of the pen."[18] And Félix Bertaux, erroneously rendering the title as *Eugenie oder die Kaiserzeit*, calls it an "intermezzo," in which Mann "evoked with quiet imaginativeness . . . the period of a bourgeoisie still flourishing but already conscious of its approaching end." [19]

It is difficult to assign a place to, or to predict the future of, this novel. Like Fontane's writings—*Effi Briest* excepted—and like *Royal Highness*, it lacks the power to assert itself among the very best. Yet it is more important than the ordinary well-written novels which each generation brings forth for its instruction and entertainment. Eventually the acceptance of *Eugenie* will probably depend on the general acceptance of Heinrich Mann as a major author. For the moment one can only say that it is the finest of the five novels written by Mann during the years of the Republic, and the only one which one can read and reread with pleasure.

In *Eugenie* Mann once more returns to the Lübeck of his earliest childhood. The plot concerns the decline of an upper middle-class couple, Consul Jürgen West and his wife Gabriele. On the surface, the Wests lead the contented life of a respectable family, but "misfortune and vice were attractive; they beckoned unhealthily." [20] Through the mysterious figure of Pidohn they are lured into adventures. Jürgen, entering into stock market speculations with Pidohn, risks and loses both his fortune and his position; Gabriele begins to lead a double life under Pidohn's influence. Restless in the alien northern German environment, she ventures into sections of the town where decent women do not go; she toys with the notion of fleeing aboard a vessel back to her native Bordeaux; and she comes dangerously close to running away with Pidohn. But in the end the tempter himself is ruined and returned to jail, while the couple, with the help of Mayor Reuter—a kind of *deus ex machina*—starts a new life in the shelter of poverty and anonymity.

This simple story line is interwoven with, and reinforced by, an elegiac playlet. During a visit to the Wests, the poet von Heines improvises a drama about Napoleon III and his wife, Eugénie. The process of invention is interrupted by platitudes from the audience, but Gabriele pursues the idea of having the play written, so that it may be staged in her villa. She goes to see the poet who, gaining insight into her problems, accedes to her wishes. His purpose, however, is not merely to please her but to cure her. In his

mind, Gabriele's character fuses with that of the Empress Eugénie, and Napoleon's with that of Pidohn. They are to play
the leading roles. The main rehearsal takes place in the middle of
the novel and the actual performance is described near the end. It
brings about the fervently hoped-for turn of events in the lives of
Consul and Mrs. West. Significantly, Pidohn has already been ar-
rested by this time, and von Heines himself takes on the role of
Napoleon, his person doing as much for the happy denouement as
does his little drama.

The triangle of Pidohn, Jürgen, and Gabriele is formed and
held together by forces which are both powerful and subtle. The
Consul cannot escape the desire to gain wealth quickly, and so he
lends his prestige to Pidohn's ruthlessness. Gabriele is attracted to
Pidohn for quite different reasons. He stirs up in her the desire
to escape a pedestrian existence and offers the means for this escape. Yet she would not have dared to seek out Pidohn if her
husband had not been linked to this sinister character. Jürgen
West knows this: "To what extent was all of this the fault of his
poor wife? To her, too, Pidohn had been a present of fate. She
had not picked him out. Undoubtedly he had been repugnant to
her, but had come closer to her only to the extent to which Jürgen
himself had made common cause with him." (160) And Pidohn,
finally, clings to the Wests as evil attaches itself to those it wants
to destroy.

Pidohn is more complex than either Jürgen or Gabriele. He is
the adventurer who longs for respectability. At the same time, he
is aware of the fact that he can never achieve it and that his main
function is to test the mettle of the bourgeoisie. "You will not have
to go along into the wild storm," he says to Gabriele. "No, things
don't go that far with people like you. In the case of accidents you
are still insured with one another. But not I, Madame; Pidohn has
insurance with no one." (78)

As a tempter Pidohn allegorically represents the principle of
radical consistency which Hermann Broch considers necessary to
"the disintegration of values." Heinrich Mann recognizes the seductive element of an ever-narrowing logic which leads to the
fragmentation of life. Broch points out that without an all-
encompassing faith mankind inevitably ends with art for art's
sake, business for business's sake, the military for the military's

sake and so on, with nothing to bridge the abyss between individuals. In *Eugenie* Heinrich Mann offers as a defense against this development a humane and understanding conservatism.

Although Jürgen West is the burgher and patrician of the novel, it is the poet von Heines through whom Heinrich Mann's conservatism is most clearly expressed. Von Heines is modeled after the poet Emmanual Geibel, "Lübeck's most famous son before Thomas Mann and one of the most dedicated prophets of German unity." [21] Heinrich's portrait of Geibel is lovingly but not uncritically drawn. Before our eyes there emerges not a great poet, but a very fine man who combines pride with modesty, who reconciles his own inner conflicts, who understands much, and who is willing to use the wisdom of his old age practically in the interest of others.

Besides being a fairly accurate picture of, and tribute to, a nineteenth century poet whom his contemporaries considered the equal of Mörike—Geibel himself knew better—Heinrich Mann's character study constitutes a fascinating analysis of the poetic mind *per se*. Von Heines endeavors to present in his poems an optimistic view of life. Yet suddenly he finds himself intrigued by the misfortune of the third Napoleon and is startled by the discovery that tragedy attracts him. Parallel to this, he can combine the loftiest thoughts with an interest in the stock market. But for all of his contradictions, or even because of them, he is and remains a man dedicated to the life of the mind. His ardent patriotism leads him to exaggerate the role he has played in the unification of Germany, but he is not a chauvinist, as two young officers find out quite unexpectedly.

"I wielded this sword like you," he said to the young warriors across from him. "I kept it pure and strong until you did the last stroke." To this, too, the officers nodded.

By themselves they doubted whether he wasn't saying too much. They had always fought their battles alone; when things became serious, the poet, at any rate, had been absent.

He refuted their thoughts on the spot. What was victory if not the fruit and the blessing of faith in our people! That faith he himself had spread. Without the idea fighting for us, where would we be!

We had that horrible example before our eyes. A war in which no intellect, no poet, also fought the fight, took his empire from our beaten opponent. He had to walk the road of misery. (29–30)

The implication is clear that a man of von Heines' integrity would not have sided with his own country in a vainglorious war.

Von Heines-Geibel is a man of tradition. This enables him to understand and judge without indignation or hatred. He does not thunder against Pidohn. He does not berate Jürgen or Gabriele West; therefore he can help them. This characteristic endears him to Heinrich Mann, who undoubtedly identifies himself somewhat with the epigonal poet. In an essay published in 1933 in Holland, Mann has this to say about the Nazis and himself:

Always I have only pitied my countrymen because of their unhappy passion to hate others merely because, presumably, they were favored by fortune. As a writer, I myself have had some contemporaries who were more successful than I. I never hated them. And if possible, I admired them. But then I am from an old family of the old Germany, and he who has tradition is guarded against false feelings. Tradition enables us to understand and makes us inclined toward skepticism and kindness. Only upstarts behave at times like barbarians.[22]

It does not seem too far-fetched to link both von Heines' and Heinrich Mann's conservatism with the latter's tolerance toward the Germans after World War II—a tolerance his brother Thomas could not muster.[23] Nor does one go wrong in assuming that the aristocratic moderation of von Heines anticipates that of Mann's Henri IV.

With *Die grosse Sache* (1930), Heinrich Mann returned to the contemporary scene, this time reducing references to the past to a bare minimum. A separate six-page essay entitled "Mein Roman" ("My Novel") furnishes a commentary to the volume, explaining its didactic purpose, the author's understanding of the younger generation, and his general attitude toward the novel as a genre.

Concerning the ingredients of the novel, Mann states in the essay: "I invented a plot. In the case of the novel this is, if not the first element, the decisive one. If one had the best characters, it would still be of no use. They need the plot by means of which they gain validity and which fits them like a tailor-made coat. Members of society are not without clothes, and the persons of a novel remain completely incomprehensible without a plot appropriate to them." [24] As regards the younger generation he says, "Others who lived in earlier times would have been downright desperate about their hopeless proletarization; not these youngsters. This generation adapts itself all right. As a substitute for real successes it has the sporting spirit. At the same time, it knows existential fear. What is going to happen when one is no longer young?—superannuated, beset by battle fatigue, and can no longer keep up the pace?" [25] And thirdly, speaking of the novel *Die grosse Sache* itself, Mann sums up his intention as follows: "With the novel *Die grosse Sache* I am pursuing one single limited purpose; it is quite non-political. Gently and on the sly I bring to the attention of our dear contemporaries that they are not only possessed by *Existenzangst*, but that perhaps they are dissatisfied on a deeper level. I attempt to let them notice that they cannot only transmit sounds and bodies through the air; their forces go further, and they dispose of another as yet too little-known apparatus. . . . We also have forces of the soul and do not know yet how far they go." [26] These comments reveal Mann's concern with being understood by everyone. He did not need to worry. The novel itself makes its point with simple and unmistakable directness.

Reinhold Birk, a fifty-seven year old engineer, has had an accident and during his hospitalization conceives of a plan to teach his children "a concrete lesson . . . so that once and for all they understand life properly." [27] He exaggerates the seriousness of his illness and confides to his sons and daughters that he has made an invention from which they may profit after his death. The invention, an explosive of tremendous power, does not really exist. But the children now proceed to exploit their father's non-existent brain-child, run into all sorts of obstacles, and finally learn, within a period of three days, that an honorable existence cannot be based on a swindle. They accept their father's homespun philosophy, which is plumply stated early in the novel: "Learn responsibility! Learn to endure! Learn to be happy!" (21)

Birk has been called "a Prospero of work." [28] This seems to be a rather oblique comparison, for Birk's misfortune does not have its origin in a specific wrong; it is a sign of the times. Before the war the engineer was famous and well-to-do. After the inflation, he was a poor and unknown technician. "At this time, celebrities re-submerged into the anonymous army of labor. Not that they were no longer mentioned or shown. But it happened now in the company of a thousand others. In pictorial layouts the journal of this industrial combine alone presented bi-weekly about seventy deserving technicians of all levels to themselves and their contemporaries." (14) While the beginnings of automation took away Birk's individuality, swindlers rose to positions of prominence. Whenever engineers rose to prominence, they ceased to be engineers. Birk realizes that he has three choices: he can either work, or exploit connections (as does his "friend" Schattich), or turn to crime like the murderer Mulle. For the sake of his dignity he chooses work, and invents the story of the explosive to teach his sons and daughters his own method of preserving his personal dignity.

In telling his pedagogical tale, Mann blends the fantastic with starkest realism and cold impersonality with great tenderness. The schemes of everyone seeking wealth through Birk's invention are fantastic. The language borrowed from the jargon of the underworld and from big-city slang is realistic. Schattich, his business associate von List, boxers, and actors exhibit an impersonal, robot-like attitude. Birk, on the other hand, guides the destiny of his children from his hospital bed without sentimentality but with gentle concern.

The central problem of the novel, that of giving the younger generation some bearings while society seems out of joint, is stated in terms which belong to a specific moment in time. *Die grosse Sache* could not be written today, just as Elmer Rice's *Imperial City* could not be repeated. There is one aspect of *Die grosse Sache* which lifts it to a level higher than that of a mere document of an era. That is the irony with which its crisp didacticism is suffused. Birk says to himself "We are supposed to work, to have children, and to die. One thing is not sadder than the other. We merely must make it endurable through resigned devotion and irony." (12)

Irony, in this instance, is not the result of doubt. It does not stem from the thought that the author could have taken a different point of view with equal validity. Its origin must rather be sought in Mann's certainty that the younger generation would not listen to him, for in a note published in 1928 the young people of the Twenties are characterized as "unhistorical." "If one hears them, six months ago no one was there as yet, and who they will be six months from now remains to be seen. They only read books which do not point beyond this era. They draw no conclusions from their experiences, and the past does not even exist as admonition and shadow. . . ." [29] A younger Heinrich Mann might have shouted this message with tones of despair. But in *Die grosse Sache* a transfiguration through age is noticeable. The author's knowledge that he is preaching to deaf ears lends his work a glow of joviality, and his sometimes banal statements the patina of wisdom.

In Thomas Mann, *Die grosse Sache* awakened memories of the time when the two brothers painted a picture book for their sisters, from the pages of which Heinrich had apparently borrowed his representative of the third way of life, the murderer Mulle. But beyond this private joke Thomas recognized and even exaggerated the virtues of the book.[30] In his summary he says: "Once more, all this is severe, even in its fun aspects, even in its kindness; severe and painful, lonely in its sociability, knowledgeable and naive, fascinating and hard to endure, touching and insulting. Like what? Like genius." [31]

In 1931 the genius of Heinrich Mann received more recognition than ever before or after. The German literary world celebrated his sixtieth birthday with speeches, laudatory articles, and testimonial dinners, the panegyrists outdoing each other in the use of superlatives, and the Prussian Academy of Arts making him president of its Literary Section. This was a propitious moment for publishing a collection of essays about those Frenchmen whom he had long regarded as his teachers, and whom he wished his countrymen to accept as theirs. For a title he chose that of a piece which has already been discussed: *Geist und Tat* ("Spirit and Action").[32]

Apart from a number of shorter studies, the volume contains essays dealing with Choderlos de Laclos, Stendhal, Hugo, Flaubert, and Zola. All except "Stendhal" had been printed before.

The emphasis on important social novelists—with the conspicuous absence of Balzac[33]—is, of course, no accident. Mann wished to use the essay form, even more than drama and fiction, to exercise an influence on his environment, and chose as subjects those men who had done for France what he had always wanted to do for Germany. In the words of Lutz Weltmann, "the concentrated spirit of this volume is action." [34]

Discussing Heinrich Mann as an essayist, Richard Exner makes a few general remarks which deserve to be noted. He grants Mann a "sense of facts," but points out that in the essays certain "basic epic traits" elevate the presentation of factual material well above the level of ordinary reportage.[35] He further points out that Mann's essays have the quality of good oratory.[36] One is inclined to speak of pedagogical oratory, for the attempt to educate is palable indeed. And thirdly, Professor Exner states that, differing in this from Hofmannsthal or Thomas Mann, he rarely uses quotations as magic or conjuring formulas, preferring to let the material cited blend into the text.[37] This is no disadvantage in the opinion of the critic, who thinks highly enough of Heinrich's ability as a writer to believe that the latter's own phrases may become quotations for others.[38]

Whereas in his appraisal Mr. Exner strikes a fair balance between form and content in Mann's essayistic work, others, like Alfred Kantorowicz, for instance, heavily stress the importance of the content, or rather, of the social criticism culled by Mann from the novels with which he deals.[39] A close examination of two essays, chronologically the first and the last of those included in *Geist und Tat*, will show a shift in Mann's concern from *Aussage* to *Ausdruck*, from statement to formulation, without loss of the ever present social message.

"Choderlos de Laclos," written in 1905, and "Stendhal," written in 1931, have certain similarities. Both were composed to bring a book and its author to the attention of the public. Both address contemporary society, "Choderlos de Laclos" that of the peaceful, slightly decadent first decade of the century; "Stendhal" that of the unsettled era following World War I. But there are also significant differences. In particular, the earlier essay, written as an introduction to Heinrich Mann's own translation of *Les liaisons*

dangereuses, begins with a discussion of the novel, a brief sketch
about its author's life being attached. In "Stendhal," on the other
hand, the emphasis is placed on the person of the artist who is
introduced first and elaborately, the second part treating—somewhat cavalierly—his novels, *Le rouge et le noir* receiving more
attention than the others, since its centenary occasioned the essay
in the first place.

With great cunning, Mann telescopes portions of the plot of
Les Liaisons Dangereuses. "A young girl, fresh from the nunnery,
is transported into the world and, with the aid of two elegant
criminals, unaware of what is happening to her, is reduced to
the lowest form of prostitution. A monster of wickedness and
naïveté is the result." This beginning arouses interest and stimu-
lates further reading. The promise of something lurid enhances
one's fascination. "She [la Merteuil] will end up with erotic
strangenesses." Mann says "strangenesses," making it sound less
clinical and more intriguing than "perversities." Who can now refuse to finish the preface and go on to perusing the novel itself?

But Choderlos de Laclos' masterpiece is not "sold" as obscene or
pornographic. Love in its various aspects is presented as applied
psychology, as dangerous adventure, and as combat. Furthermore, the essayist sees in it the vehicle which carries the ideological freight of the novel, which he understands to be at once sociological, philosophical, and historical.

Mann maintains that the particular forms which the relationships
of the sexes assume in the eighteenth century novel are the consequence of leisure. The "good" society before the French Revolution avoids boredom by cruel erotic games. But these do not lead
to happiness. Choderlos de Laclos proves to be a moralist when
he has his "brilliant seducer" Valmont say, "I am outraged . . .
when I think that this man, without reflection, without making
the slightest effort, simply by stupidly following the dictates of his
heart, finds a bliss which I cannot attain." Valmont here condemns
himself, condemns lewdness, and even condemns reason.

Concerning the philosophy of Laclos' protagonist, Mann singles
out another of Valmont's statements, which is Kantian in spirit,
though the French soldier-author could not possibly have read
Kant. "I am tempted to believe that those who are called virtuous

are not so deserving as one likes to tell us," says Valmont. He has found out that pleasure can be derived from virtuous acts, and he concludes that virtue which pursues an aim is not meritorious. Like Kant he believes that merit accrues from abiding by a principle. But most un-Kantian, his principle is amoral. For him, as Mann says, "the difficulty of a thing is always the decisive factor." That means that the challenge is not in the idea but in the obstacle. And here Valmont becomes modern. Glorifying the difficult as such leads to pride in achievements, regardless of their nature, as long as they are not within reach of the ordinary person. A new cult of individualism is born. Valmont's alienation from society marks the beginning of a process which culminates in the estheticism of the *fin de siècle*.

Mann briefly notes the steps of this process. He points out that Valmont does not yet suffer from his solitude, as his successors do. There is a direct line from him to Chateaubriand, Musset, Flaubert, and Maupassant. The isolation originating in a rebellion against society, it is asserted, changes to a painful knowledge of one's loneliness, and finally to "the tragedy of every soul described by Maupassant—loneliness which one tries in vain to break down; loneliness which one bears with gentlemanly disdain."

Historically, the decline of social consciousness is paralleled by a decline of personal vigor. Mann boldly states, "A salon in the middle of the eighteenth century is a run-down republic of the fifteenth." He quotes the seducer: " 'Once I have achieved this triumph, I shall shout at my rivals: Look at my work and try to find a second one equal to it in our century.' " And then he adds, "A Roman could speak this way when he had conquered half a continent; a condottiere, after his eventual entry into a town on which he had had a deceitful eye for years. The Caesar of the eighteenth century makes his announcement in anticipation of a woman's defeat."

Mentioning the affinity which exists between the author of *Im Schlaraffenland* and the author of *Les liaisons dangereuses,* Kantorowicz claims that the former rediscovered for Germany Laclos the social critic.[40] This is quite true but hardly exhaustive. It has already been shown that the essay evinces Mann's appreciation of the psychologist Laclos. It should now be added that he does not ignore Laclos the writer who, after all, wrote a novel and not a treatise:

The emphatic epistolary style of *The New Heloïse* is far away; here is present the trenchancy without images of *Candide* and the *Essai sur les moeurs*. Rapid action; incisive reflection . . . The book is clever and deep; as unassailable in its outer mechanics [*der äußeren Mache*] as in the play of its mainsprings within.

Thus Mann's rediscovery of Laclos is also that of one artist by another, albeit not so eminent a one as Stendhal.

Stendhal is presented as a man who deserves to be heard in pre-Hitler Germany. What makes him modern is the similarity of his situation with that prevailing in the Weimar Republic shortly before its unhappy end. He was "a son of a dissolute society and a war, irreverent, and resolved to make his way either by force and adventurously or through middle class methods. . . . He nurtured hatred for the older generation. . . . He took his age and its conditions matter-of-factly. . . . He felt the need to keep in furious motion and to obey a self-chosen leader without reservation." These are his credentials as an individual who has the right to address Mann's contemporaries.

But the nineteenth century French novelist has his roots in eighteenth century ideology. This, according to Mann, was fortunate, for it gave him distance and perspective. It allowed him to write novels which reveal how money perverted the Revolution:

They [the speculators] made money on his [Napoleon's] glorious deeds; he hated them but could not rid himself of them; they regarded him fundamentally as their tool. The Revolution received a fascist turn from capital—in those days already; and ever after, when capital needed the postponement of democratic realizations, what came to the fore again? The monkeys of Napoleon.

Stendhal opposed the "monkeys" and sided with the Emperor, who appreciated Corneille and thought more highly of his legal code than of his forty victories.

Viewing the post-Napoleonic world from the vantage point of an eighteenth century philosophy gave Stendhal an intellectual

nobility which Mann finds missing in the romantics. Stendhal
understood love and truthfulness. Therefore he recognized the
lack of true love and the hypocrisy of his era. Only Victor Hugo,
so the essayist asserts, occasionally rivaled him in this. But Hugo
was less lonely. Loneliness and obscurity were the price which
Stendhal had to pay for his independence from society and from
criticism.

In "Stendhal," the identification of Mann with his subject is less
pronounced than it is in "Zola," but more strongly evident than in
the Laclos essay. Mann especially feels that Henri Beyle shared
his ideas concerning the mission of the writer. His French mentor,
so he avers, "did not write while serving Napoleon." This is proof
to him that writing can readily be replacd by doing; that, in fact,
it is but a poor substitute for doing. "A person properly employed
does not need to reflect about himself," he says. "The world from
which he does not suffer does not stimulate him to make a riposte.
Words and sentences are, among other things, also a defense; a
perfectly happy age would have no literature."

The point made here is tenuous. Many poets and writers would
not agree with Heinrich Mann. Homer, Shakespeare, and Goethe
would certainly differ. Schiller, on the other hand, would readily
consent and classify Mann the way he classified himself, namely
as *sentimentalisch,* that is to say, as one of those whose creativity
stems solely from their insights into the disparity between the real
and the ideal world.

Turning to Stendhal's novels in the second part of his essay,
Mann deals summarily with *La Chartreuse de Parme* and *Lucien
Leuwen,* concentrating essentially on *Le rouge et le noir.* The
interpretation of this masterpiece and its hero contains nothing
unusual. Mann calls it the story "of a great but suppressed
power." Julien Sorel, born too late to be a soldier under Napoleon,
must needs be at odds with the order in which he is forced to live,
and it is evidently the order rather than he which is on trial. Since
there is no other avenue for a talented young man of bourgeois
origin to rise above his humble station, Sorel becomes a priest, but
without faith. He becomes the secretary of a high official while
hating the system served by his master. He becomes the lover of
the official's daughter, who looks down on him as a hired hand.
His passionate desire to succeed is counteracted by his shyness

and despair, so that he experiences the fiercest emotional turmoil. By the time he commits murder he has lost all self-esteem. The act of killing another person "is a kind of voluntary death into which he merely took gentle Madame Rênal along"; and his end under the Guillotine constitutes the exclamation point at the conclusion of "the most formidable accusation ever to be leveled against an age."

Mann recapitulates the story of Julien Sorel for the benefit of the younger generation in search for a bearing at the beginning of the Great Depression. To the writer, *Le rouge et le noir* offers another lesson: "Social novels, the memorabilia of an epoch, can be handled only with simplicity, which is exactly what is hard to find." The novel as "'a mirror on a highway'" organizes that which seems fortuitous and without connection, and gives it a meaning that can be understood a hundred years hence. This lesson is immediately applied to the essay. The vocabulary of "Stendhal" hardly exceeds that of a high school student. The only nearly untranslatable foreign word which occurs in it is the word *"cicisbeo,"* the context making its meaning sufficiently clear. There is not much imagery. Inpressionist aperçus are introduced sparingly and, like the following example, explained beforehand: "Several women climb down, fully alive, from the frames of old paintings. Mademoiselle de la Mole resembles Judith; blond Madame de Rênal is painted by Correggio." There are no contrived sentences. Simplicity prevails, indeed.

But it is a deceptive simplicity, for the essay possesses the luminosity of a string of pearls. This must be attributed to the perfect construction of the individual paragraphs, each of which is self-contained and yet related to its neighbors. Almost every paragraph is built around a contrast, but the contrasts, unlike those of *Die Göttinnen,* which hold each other in check, make one another stand out in relief. Stendhal's hatred for his father and the first erotic impressions received from his mother mark the beginning. Then follow other pairs: fortune and misfortune, grocery and army, energy and dull cloudy days, the Moscow fire and a volume of Voltaire, writing and doing, freedom and plutocracy, romanticism and the sobriety of the Code Napoleon, honor and trickery; one might go on listing examples from every page. Interpolations of the present tense in the narrative past reinforce the various juxtapositions; and finally there are the last three paragraphs of the first part, which begin with the present perfect tense, summarizing with a tone of finality some of the points the pedagogical orator Mann wishes to hammer home.

Stendhal was one of the godfathers of the essay concerning him, but Flaubert, so it appears, was another. In his study of Flaubert and George Sand, written in 1905, Mann allows the author of *Madame Bovary* to reflect about himself and say, among other things:

I remember how my heart beat, and what violent pleasure I experienced when I contemplated a wall of the Akropolis (the one to the left, when one goes up to the Propylees). And I ask myself, if a book, independently from what it says, cannot produce the same effect. Does not the exactness of verbal architecture, the rarity of its constituent parts, the smoothness of the surface, the harmony of the whole contain an inner virtue, a kind of divine power, an eternal principle?

The Stendhal essay, more than "Choderlos de Laclos," bears testimony to the fact that Mann never quite lost sight of the true nature of art and that, in the midst of many preoccupations, he was able to write the finest prose if his subject matter inspired him sufficiently.

The third of the moralizing contemporary novels expressing optimism, *Ein ernstes Leben* (1932) is also the last work of Heinrich Mann's "second phase," that is to say, the last longer work of fiction prior to his forced emigration. For this reason, and also because it is in part the story of Mann's second wife, Nelly Kroeger, one critic at least discusses it in a tone of sentimental reverence.[41] But except for the early chapters written with classic simplicity, even a devotee of the author cannot recommend the book. It is a hodge-podge, and if it is mentioned here at all, that is only because the ingredients of the melange reveal Heinrich Mann to be a man very much attuned to his time.

Marie Lehning, a farm laborer's daughter from the shores of the Baltic Sea, is drawn into a most adventurous life by a pair of sinister twins from Berlin. Fundamentally good and innocent, she has an illegitimate son, descends from seamstress and field-hand to bar-lady, and becomes involved in theft, kidnapping, and even murder. Through a kindly police inspector she escapes the web of circumstantial evidence which had been spun around her and returns to a simple life, finding happiness with a childhood friend. In other words, the novel moves from a fine description of a childhood in poverty to the soap-operatic, and from there into the mediocrity of a detective story.

The mixture of styles corresponds to a mixture of elements echoing other contemporary works. Marie Lehning wants to be good but cannot. "Doch die Verhältnisse, sie sind nicht so." [42] She is the victim of a rapidly decaying age symbolized by the big city —like Döblin's Bieberkopf. The bar belonging to Adele Fuchs is reminiscent of the bistros depicted by Erich Kästner, whose Mr. and Mrs. Moll are counterparts to Mann's Ignaz and Vicky Bäuerlein; Vicky's attempt to take Marie's child away from her is seen by Herbert Ihering as a parallel to motives from Hauptmann's *Ratten (The Rats)* [43] and, finally, Inspector Kirsch is a literary ancestor of Dürrenmatt's Inspector Bärlich.

Reading *Ein ernstes Leben,* one gains the impression that the author recognized many signs of the times but was unable to deal with them in novelistic form. No plot, no life, no single character lent itself to the representation of the turmoil on the market place or the mood of the masses. Mann drew the consequences from his failure: he abandoned the social novel. With the end of the Weimar Republic in sight, he summarized once more the errors of his age and uttered his last warnings against Hitler in a major essay entitled "Bekenntnis zum Übernationalen"—it appeared in the December 1932 issue of *Die Neue Rundschau*—and then he fixed his attention on a historical novel. But this was during his next period, one marked by a gentle skepticism not dissimilar to that of his inspector Kirsch.

CHAPTER 6

The Skeptic

WITH the advent of the Third Reich it became impossible for Heinrich Mann to remain in Germany. His voice, one of the strongest and most respected among those opposing the new regime, had to be silenced immediately by the Hitlerites. On February 15, 1933, he was expelled from the Prussian Academy of Arts and Sciences,[1] and soon thereafter he left for France.[2]

In contrast with many other refugees he did not settle in Paris, but rather chose Nice and Bandol near Toulon as his domicile. But, then, he did not consider himself a refugee. He had known and loved France for many years, and he was known and loved there. He participated in public life by writing articles for Albert Sarraut's *Dépêche de Toulouse;* by being active in the *Front Populaire;* and by working in behalf of a German Popular Front.[3] And he had an imposing literary project under way. This project, although begun earlier in Germany, needed the French atmosphere for a successful completion, since it was a two-volume novel about Henri IV of France. In a letter to Klaus Pinkus in 1938 he wrote about its genesis:

Therefore I first finished my novel; it is to appear next month. Repeatedly people tried to hurry me, but I really think that I worked quickly enough—800 large printed pages in 2½ years. If one adds the first part, the whole "Henri" has fourteen hundred printed pages. I first intended to write it ten years ago. I brought some preliminary studies and the first pages with me from Berlin. The entire period of emigration up to now had this content for me.[4]

And later he wrote, "*Henri Quatre,* eight years of a sojourn in France, in those days called exile. Formerly the terms were visit and trip. It was the exile which was fruitful."[5] Fruitful, indeed, for the epic about the first Bourbon king is a masterly piece of historical fiction rivalling the very best of its genre.

The preoccupation with a historical figure meant three things to the author. First, it meant the acquisition of new knowledge and new symbols. Secondly, it meant a return to the Renaissance and the revision of earlier notions about it. And thirdly, it meant an escape from the unpleasantnesses of the contemporary scene.

It should be noted parenthetically that Mann was not the only German writer in the 'thirties to flee into the past from the chaotic events of the day. Reviewing *Die Jugend des Königs Henri Quatre* (trans. as *Young Henry of Navarre*) in 1938, Georg Lukacs was able to point out that "the historical novel has moved more and more into the center of production of the anti-fascist emigration from Germany . . . ." [6] But within Germany too, a large number of novelists treated historical subjects at the time. A Nazi history of literature such as that by Norbert Langer contains a sizable section on historical fiction, although it does not even include Werner Bergengruen or Jochen Klepper. Mann simply shared the mood of many. Only, his choice of a hero was more felicitous than that of his colleagues; his vision went beyond "the idea of the Reich" (Beumelburg) or "pietism as a force in statecraft" (Klepper); and he knew how to write.

The plot of the Henri Quatre novel is history itself. Through the eyes of the prince who had to conquer his kingdom inch by inch and battle by battle, the reader sees unfold before him the panorama of a strife-torn nation. All layers of society are represented; peasants, craftsmen, merchants, common soldiers, priests, poets, lawyers, noblemen, and kings. All major events of Henri's life are depicted; the victories of Ivry and Arques, the bloody night of St. Bartholomew, the peace with Spain at Vervins, Henri's entry into Paris, and the Edict of Nantes are perhaps the most important ones. But the whole is greater than the sum of its parts. The second half of the sixteenth century in Western Europe is resuscitated here. On a gigantic stage moderation struggles with fanaticism, and kindness is temporarily victorious over malevolence.

This drama gains much from not being entirely objective. The author makes it clear that he does not wish to compete with historiographers. He uses his source material freely. That is to say, he

inserts phrases and sentences into his narrative which are ver-
batim translations from Montaigne's essays, from letters by Henri
and his mother, and from various memoirs. At the same time he
does not hesitate to distort history. For example, the flight of
Henri II to Bordeaux seems to be a figment of Mann's imagination. All three encounters of Henri IV with Montaigne are fictitious; and the latter's account of his conversation with Michelangelo constitutes an outright anachronism. However, such falsifica-
tions do not negatively affect the overall picture of the times, and
are justified by the author's purposes in the same sense in which
Schiller's and Goethe's violations of history are justified in *Don
Carlos* and *Egmont*, for instance.[7]

Whereas no one has taken exception to the deviations from the
written records of the past, annoyance and regret have been expressed regarding another kind of liberty taken by Mann, namely
that of drawing parallels between the League and the Hitlerian
movement.[8] The analogies undeniably exist, and they are bluntly
obvious. The preacher Boucher owes much to Joseph Goebbels,
and Henri Guise resembles the Führer himself, while the Duke of
Mayenne exhibits Goering's physique and Laval's mind.[9] But it
appears that Mann did not borrow traits from his notorious contemporaries in order to make his novel sensationally timely. Even
the idea of the recurrent in history, expressed in his autobiography,[10] must be regarded as an afterthought. For he certainly did
not see any parallel between Hitler's usurpation of power and
Henri's peaceful entry into Paris. Yet he used Hitler's favorite
term *Machtergreifung* (seizure of power) as heading for the
chapter dealing with Henri's bloodless conquest of his capital. It is
safe to assume—and totally non-political analogies bear this out[11]
—that the author simply drew on his experiences in order to
breathe life into his characters. His method might disturb older
critics, but already there exists a generation of readers who are
not reminded of the Third Reich by such words as *Arbeitsdienst*
(labor service) or *Gauleiter* (district leader), and who can relish
Mann's vivid descriptions without being troubled by obtrusive as-
sociations.

In a few respects Heinrich Mann had a model for his hero also,
namely, himself. Ulrich Weisstein says,

To the fugitive from the Louvre, La Rochelle is "a city of benevolence and safety," just as Paris was to his [the fugitive's] creator in 1933. French is for both of them "the language [of their] choice," which is evident, as far as Heinrich Mann is concerned, from the *moralités* attached to the individual chapters. And the author's assertion about his hero that he became "a better writer the more he learned to act with greatness, the one for the sake of the other . . ." corresponds fully to his own ideal.[12]

To this should be added that Mann's affinity for his principal character might have been less, if Henri had not been an aristocrat. In the *moralité* to chapter VII—only the first volume has, by way of summary, French *moralités* at the end of each chapter—a special point is made of the fact that Henri is not "hard and cruel as is generally the case with those who rise from the bottom. But that is just the point. He does not come from below. He only goes through the condition of the humble." (VI, 549) One is reminded of the poet von Heines in *Eugenie* and of Mann's pride in his own patrician background expressed in *Der Hass* ("Hatred").[13]

Even more than a historical novel, the two tomes under consideration may be regarded as a biography. They tell the story of an unusual man from his early childhood to his maturity and untimely death. All characters, events, and landscapes have a meaning only with regard to Henri of Navarre. The author's spotlight is trained on him; the others partake of it only insofar as they enter his sphere of activity. Henri's bias is the author's bias, much to the detriment of some historical personages, but not to the detriment of the work.

Henri, as he is described, appears as an illustration of Goethe's words about Iphigenia, "All human frailty is redeemed by pure humanity." Henri combines a quick grasp of the demands of the moment with vision; simplicity with shrewdness, and kindness with strength. At times he makes serious mistakes; he fails to foresee some of the consequences of his deeds; he is duped, and he deceives in turn. Chance, a most potent force, sometimes favors him and sometimes hurts or frustrates him. But because of his inherent goodness he is always loved and understood by the people. Only the extremists, be they Huguenots or Catholics, partisans of the Valois or of Philip of Spain, vilify him. And because of his strength he prevails in the end.

By contrast, his antagonists are painted just a trifle blacker, and perhaps less complex, than they really were. Philip II, the Guise, and the Catholic Church do not fare very well in the novel, and Catherine of Medici "does not receive her historical due in Heinrich Mann," [14] as Lukacs rightly points out. Her efforts and those of her chancellor L'Hôpital—the latter is not even mentioned—to break the dominance of the Guise and to strengthen the absolute monarchy in France have no place in a work designed to glorify Henri, and Henri alone. Lukacs recognizes this as being inherent "in the biographical form of the historical novel," [15] and regards it as a weakness. But it is questionable whether complete fairness and historical accuracy would have yielded as memorable a figure as Mann's Henri or as impressive a message as Mann's gospel of moderation and reason.

Henri's road is that of a naïve, morally healthy, and very sensual individual who is constantly threatened both by the vicious world around him and by his own inner conflict between passion and reason. Though a good practical psychologist, he never arrives at the self-knowledge for which he strives, and he never achieves equanimity. He acts and suffers, but he is strong and humble, "prince of royal blood" and "people." Therefore he can, in spite of himself, become one of the two "administrators of the humanitarian heritage." [16]

The other one is Montaigne. Montaigne teaches Henri to recognize some of the principles by which one must live, and by which Henri intuitively wishes to live. The words of the great essayist have a clarifying and liberating effect upon the prince. May he understand ever so little about his own character, Montaigne's precepts he knows to be right and part of his nature. In an age dominated by cruelty and self-interest, the philosopher familiarizes Henri with the Ciceronian statement that nothing makes one as popular as kindness; "nihil est tam populare quam bonitas." He also gives him the classical formulation of skepticism with his famous "que sais-je," which, however, does not imply moral relativism. It merely refers to metaphysics and religion, enabling Henri later to say, "God . . . is bored with matters of faith." (VII, 205) And thirdly Montaigne teaches Henri moderation, moderation even with regard to goodness; for any excessive zeal turns right into wrong. With these precepts, repeated often throughout the novel both in German and in French, the prince destined to unify France is able to fulfill his mission and to become "Seul roi de qui le pauvre ait gardé la mémoire"—the only king who still lives today among the poor.

Henri's struggle for peace and unity against greed and obscurantism takes place at a given time in history and in a specific geographical location. But the author succeeds in elevating it to the level of a parable. It is not a struggle which can be fully won; nor can it be hopelessly lost. It is the labor of Sisyphus, the war "that never ceases." (VII, 745)[17] What permanent triumph there is, is solely Mann's, who, presenting the eternal conflict between good and evil, has made virtue more appealing than vice.

History, biography, parable, the three planes of the novel necessitate three corresponding levels of time. For the historical fiction there is historical time marked by dates and an orderly sequence of events. For the biography there is Henri's subjective experience of time. And for the parable there is simultaneity and timelessness. The first of these demands no special technique. History itself furnishes outline and plan. But the other two need devices which, if they are well employed, fulfill more than one function. Mann's devices are well employed.

Henri may, at some moments, be overwhelmed by the suddenness with which he must act, or he may suffer the agonies of waiting. Seconds labor on, and years may vanish in a flash. The author manages to recreate Henri's sense of time by accelerations and retardations noticeable in the extensions and contractions of descriptive passages and even in the varying pace of individual sentences. Time is also made to slow down, when a seemingly irrelevant episode interrupts the flow of events, as for instance the brief chapter telling how Philip II of Spain contracts a venereal disease. And perhaps the most important method by which time is made to creep or to fly is that of anticipation and reminiscence.

The chapter on Philip II, is not, of course, extraneous to the novel. Inserted between a scene at the British court with the great Elizabeth in the focus of attention, and one in which Henri prepares for his necessary conversion to Catholicism, the episode about the Spanish monarch becomes symbolic for the decay of an empire which may look strong to the world, but which is so rotten from within that it will never again dominate France or any part of the European continent. There are many other disease symbols woven into the fabric of the narrative,[18] but here it suffices to point out the dual purpose of an interlude as both a metaphor and a determinant of time.

Anticipation and reminiscence function in a similar way. From the prediction of Henri's eventual role in history by Nostradamus (VI, 49) to the last recollection of a good deed once done and a good meal once eaten by Henri (VII, 881), there are numerous instances in which Henri recalls the past to others or remembers it in silence. And usually he does so with a remark concerning either the swiftness of time or the enormity of intervals which have accommodated a multitude of occurrences. Likewise there are frequent references to the future. "He was eighteen, then. With forty years and a gray beard, wise and sly, he was to have conquered it" [Paris]. (VI, 136) Or: "When later he actually did rule, both his insight and his hatred had mightily increased." (VI, 407) In this way forecast and remembrance place sidereal time on a Procrustean bed.

Henri's memory, evident also in his repetition of words and phrases once learned, further serves as a means of establishing his identity. Often he asks, directly and indirectly, "Who am I?" He never arrives at any real certainty, but he knows that he is what he does. He rejects the epithet "great" for himself, when he realizes that he will not achieve his ultimate objective of a League of Nations. At each step he looks within himself to learn more about the core of his being. Successes and failures fill the vessel of his existence and make up his personality. At the same time he believes in God and seeks to make his life the fulfillment of His wishes. He lives without "dread," and yet one is probably not far off the mark if one sees in him a religious existentialist, fortunately possessing a character which keeps him, in Flaubert's phrase, "dans le vrai."

The many forward and backward glances, the echoes and reverberations of past and future events, do as much to express Henri's subjective experience of time as they do to lift his life out of time. A simultaneity is achieved which turns the hero into an Everyman. This aspect of the novel is supported by certain sentences which, in their universal wisdom, stated in the perennial present, sound like proverbs. A few examples will give the tenor of many:

What profits the community always breeds the mistrust that far out-
runs gratitude.   (VII, 331)
Sovereignty in the guise of homeliness is neither understood nor par-
doned.   (VII, 356)
The victories of a man are just as many temptations.   (VII, 471)

And what the epigrams leave undone is completed by the final
"Allocution" written in French. In it, at the end of the novel the
dead Henri sums up for all posterity the meaning of his earthly
existence, saying among other things, "Va, mon petit frère d'un
moment, tu me ressembles étrangement." (VII, 784) Everyman
resembles every man.

A book which tells of the lives of men both from their point of
view and *sub specie aeternitatis* must take everything seriously,
while at the same time showing the relative insignificance and
vanity of human endeavor. The Henri volumes do this magnifi-
cently. Heinrich Mann endows his hero with a keen understanding of the conflict between goodness and political action, and with
an awareness of human frailty and temporality. Henri is allowed
to laugh at himself, but the high and mighty who believe that
they can govern the destiny of the world for millennia are often
shown planning and scheming and then ridiculed with devastating sarcasm. For instance, when Catherine de Medici and the
Duke of Alba leave the room, having just concluded their sinister
deliberations, their departure is described in four words: "He
stalked; she waddled."

Needless to say, all devices, utilized by the author with excellent control over his subject matter, serve well to hold the reader's
interest from the beginning to the last page of the tremendous
work. There is no tedium. One eagerly follows the story; looks
forward with impatience to the next incident, and one is never
disappointed. And no one can lay aside the second volume after
finishing the last sentence without retaining a vivid picture of
man's enduring greatness, exemplified by a king whose death
marked a turning point in European history.

CHAPTER 7

The Backward Glance

I *Minor Efforts*

IN 1940 the German Wehrmacht invaded France, and once more Heinrich Mann had to flee. The aging author succeeded in escaping across the Pyrenees and in making his way, via Lisbon and New York, to California. Here providence granted him another decade of life and labor, but under far less favorable conditions than those which had prevailed in France. The inveterate European, now a septuagenarian, did not feel at home in the United States. His English was not as good as his French. He had no money and was virtually unknown. His friends were few, and they were refugees themselves. But even if he had had influential sponsors, the war would have prevented the foreign guest from taking part in public debates. In a letter to Klaus Pinkus dated April, 1942, he described his situation in the following words:

Here one drags one's life along without particular necessity. No one asks you to give evidence of your presence, unless it be the tax collector; and being forced to labor in the void, one is almost ashamed of the works which, under different circumstances, could have touched the living. One must not be discouraged. The situation of people like me is probably not much different in other countries. We are more or less buried under the debris of a decrepit humanity which nevertheless is in wild rebellion.[1]

The picture is one of extreme isolation[2] faced by the author with a strange mixture of resignation and optimism. "He was too reasonable to despair," a friend of his says.[3] The same ambivalence expressed in the letter speaks from the works of Mann's American decade.

Altogether Heinrich Mann wrote five, or rather four and one half, books after 1940. *Lidice* appeared in 1943 in Mexico; *Ein Zeitalter wird besichtigt* came out in 1945 in Stockholm; *Der*

Atem ("The Breath") was published in 1949 in Amsterdam; and *Empfang bei der Welt* ("Reception in The World") and the fragment *Die traurige Geschichte Friedrichs des Grossen* ("The Sad Story of Frederick the Great") were printed posthumously in East Berlin, in 1956 and 1958 respectively. These dates, however, do not represent the sequence in which the works were written. *Empfang bei der Welt* was finished in 1943, and *Der Atem* in 1947. The figure of Frederick II of Prussia occupied the author from 1940 until 1948. During these years he developed twenty-two scenes and an outline for the remainder, set down some of his ideas in a separate essay,[4] but then lost interest in the subject.

Lidice and the Frederick fragment are novels in dialogue form. Neither is memorable. *Lidice* deals with the annihilation of a Czech town by that name in retaliation for the murder of one of Hitler's cruelest henchmen. It was written as a token of gratitude for a man—Masaryk—and a country whose kindness had been a great help to Heinrich Mann in very trying days.[5] But the token was not well received, and Mann had no illusions concerning its merits. "The disapproval of the Czechs, including those capable of judgment, kept me from seeking wide distribution for the novel," he wrote to Karl Lemke in 1949. "Please, speak of *Lidice* with reserve, as a kind of secret, and mention it only in the biography and nowhere else." [6] One gladly fulfills the author's wish.

As regards the Frederick novel, it must be remembered that one is dealing with an incomplete manuscript not approved by Mann for publication. In 1946 Thomas Mann mentioned the "epic-dramatic scenes which—surprising choice of subject matter—retell in dialogue form the life of the Prussian Frederick." [7] Thomas' surprise was undoubtedly a pleasant one. He had used the dialogue form himself in his early years when he wrote his little-known *Fiorenza*. And he had dealt with the best-known king of Prussia in 1914. His brother's "epic-dramatic scenes" confirmed the affinity between two writers who, except for a few years, had felt close to each other and had watched each other's progress with satisfaction. But an inspection of the scenes completed, of the outline, and of the essay makes it clear that Heinrich's Frederick is not Thomas' Frederick. To Heinrich, the most famous of the Hohenzollerns appears as the opposite of his Henri Quatre. The latter conquered frustrations; the former nursed them. The latter loved his people and his country; the former despised his. And the king of France sought goodness, whereas the Prussian sought personal fame. Therefore Henri left behind an idea—the idea of a marriage between power and spirit—and a thriving kingdom, whereas Frederick merely left a name and a legend, his torn kingdom having vanished from the earth.

As an afterthought to his beautiful piece of historical fiction, the Frederick novel could not, in the words of Ulrich Weisstein, have "scaled the heights of the two volumes of the Henri Quatre," [8] even if it had been completed. The very conception of it was wrong in its one-sidedness. Frederick emerges as a simulator and "comedian"—a true ancestor of William II as depicted in *Der Untertan*, and this is a falsification of the basic nature of Prussianism. It is no wonder that the finished scenes are uneven; that those depicting Frederick's father stand out as effective in their Wedekind-like grotesqueness, while those dealing with Prince Frederick border on the tedious. Nor is it astonishing that Mann left the work a fragment. Nothing about it was sufficiently stimulating to overcome the onsetting lassitude of a man approaching eighty. For the review and summation of the author's life one must turn to the other three books of his last period of creativity.

Ein Zeitalter wird besichtigt is a book of memoirs, but only a small portion of its five hundred pages is autobiographical. Mann fits himself into the context of European history, usually referring to himself in the third person. History, in turn, is seen as a series of events leading up to the present, the most important phenomenon of which is the monstrous Third Reich. The author's antagonism toward Hitler largely determines the tenor of his survey, those passages dealing with his own experiences or with the lives and works of his friends being exceptions.

Mann's bias leads him to oversimplifications. His keen criticism of the German romantic soul—held responsible for many modern ills—is combined with praise for the French and Russian revolutions which are depicted as unromantic and humanitarian. By way of reinforcing his arguments, he uses Stalin's Russia as an example of a state in which justice prevails. Peter Blachstein's critique

[115]

is justified. Mann "does not fight for freedom, justice, and truth at all times and everywhere." [9] But Mann also expresses admiration for Churchill and De Gaulle—a fact noted with disapproval by his East German editors.[10] He may, therefore, be accused of a surfeit of credulity and lack of judgment, but he cannot be imputed with any other bias than a fervent anti-Hitlerianism.

A failure as a source book for political scientists, the *Zeitalter* proves a beautiful document regarding its author. One aspect of his personality in particular, his gentle agnosticism, emerges more clearly from its pages than from all of his other writings. In a chapter entitled, "A Decisive Question: God," he makes some penetrating observations concerning the godlessness of fascism and then tells the following episode from his own life which may also serve as a further example of his style:

A monk on a dusty road in the Tyrol, along which we were wandering together, seemed curious about my religion, as if it could have imparted instruction to him. "Your Reverence, none."—"You do not believe."—"That would be too much for me. To deny God one would need a self-confidence which I should find justified by nothing."—"You believe!"—"I do not deny; that is all I can do. I confess my ignorance."

He reflected. "But that is pride," he said. To my statement that I considered myself modest: "You want to be modest. You are not simple." Whereupon the Capuchin began to tell from his practice with simple people—and also with the less simple who became so only through grace. "Is grace something simple?" I asked. He was silent. We spoke of other things. When taking leave, he said suddenly, "Now I shall have to pray for you always."

The monk has stopped praying long ago. But if something that happened to me was marvelous, then this: in a monastery and on the way to a farmer's sickbed concern is being shown for a soul completing its course, and it is supposed to be mine.[11]

It must have been passages like this one which caused Thomas Mann to ignore his brother's errors in political judgment and to call the *Zeitalter* "an autobiography as criticism of an age experienced, of indescribably severe and serene splendor, naïve wisdom, and moral dignity; written in a prose whose intellectually resilient simplicity makes it appear to me as the language of the future." [12]

II *The Legacy*

In contrast to the quasi-autobiography which, in spite of its historical perspective, is still of this world, *Empfang bei der Welt* and *Der Atem* are novels written by a man who anticipates death and watches his own transfiguration. His age and solitude make his existence a living grave from which he speaks as Henri Quatre speaks from the clouds in his final *Allocution*. He feels at liberty to set down his wisdom and his admonitions, and to furnish his credentials for these without concessions to his readers. At best he addresses a select few who must be polyglot, be at home in European culture, and must know his *oeuvre* to benefit from his words.

In *Empfang bei der Welt*, French, English, or Italian words and phrases occur on the average on every third page. In *Der Atem*, only French is used, but proportionately more of it. Interestingly enough, one does not need to understand the excursions into the non-German tongues in order to follow either novel. But only the linguist knows this, while monolingual Germans cannot help but feel that they are missing something and are likely to lay aside the books with dismay.

Empfang bei der Welt is essentially an account rendered of the cultural influences which its author acknowledges to have been important in his life, and of his own contribution to European culture. One of its characters, the representative of the middle generation, is called Arthur, after Schopenhauer. This proves to be pure irony since *nomen* is anything but *omen*, Arthur being a man with a lust for life and a lust for money. At Grandfather Balthasar's ghostly banquet, music by Meyerbeer is heard. Fragments and paraphrases of lines by Hofmannsthal, Goethe, Kant, and Platen occur throughout the text and are assumed to be known. An orchestra made up of men imitating Wagner, Verdi, Brahms, Berlioz, Debussy, Chopin, Tschaikowsky, and Mozart plays Ravel's "Bolero" and Puccini's *Manon*. Photographs of Bismarck and Hitler are mentioned. " 'Si pùo?' asked André like the 'prologue' in *Pagliacci* . . . ." (241) " 'Je n'ai pas un théâtre: j'ai un bordel',— Arthur can say the same as the director of blond Nana." (243) The allusions are infinite.

And in their midst the connoisseur detects the references to Mann's own works. "In his two late novels," says Lorenz Winter,

"one observes Heinrich Mann building his own memorial statue
. . . . Titles and figures of earlier books were cited, and allusions
to himself were used so freely that there came about a very system of concordances between the author's old testament and the
new." [13] An excellent illustration of Winter's remarks may be found
in the hunchbacked singer Tamburini, whom Hermann Kesten has
declared "the best realized figure . . . a character worthy of the
best in *Die Göttinnen*." [14] This Tamburini has the same name as a
monsignor in *Die Göttinnen*, shares his physique and voice with
Sturbanotte in "Die Branzilla," and, in *Empfang bei der Welt*, is
said to have created the role of Piero in "Povera Tonietta," remembered from *Die kleine Stadt*.

Thomas Mann called *Empfang bei der Welt* "a spooky social
satire whose scene is everywhere and nowhere." [15] This is a fair
description. Physically the scene is in an undefined America—Hol-
lywood, perhaps—with highways and automobiles, references to
Roosevelt, baseball players, whisky, ice cream, and radio advertis-
ing. But intellectually all characters and events are European. The
locale has no significance.

Nor does the plot. Individual episodes are important, but not
the story. An actors' agent by the name of Arthur wants to build
a huge opera house. Through his friendship with Melusine
Barber, formerly an opera singer and now co-owner of a nearly
bankrupt bank, he brings together, at an enormous party, many
financiers who are to help him in his project. The party occupies
about half of the novel. The rest concerns Arthur's father Balthasar and the representatives of the younger generation. Balthasar is
over ninety, displays no interest in the hustle and bustle of life—
herein resembling Heinrich Mann—and feels closer to his grand-
son André and Melusine's daughter Stephanie than he does to his
energetic son. But Balthasar is not simple. With regard to money
his feelings are ambivalent. He despises it and yet hoards gold in
barrels in his cellar, reveling in it like Balzac's Father Grandet. He
approves of André's and Stephanie's mutual affection and eventually leaves all of his wealth to them. But the young people are
willing to work for their livelihood, to do without grandfather's
gold, and to turn their fortune over to Arthur and Melusine, the
eternal "hustlers."

Those who look for a moral or a summary statement about

human existence in this novel will be disappointed. Every single pronouncement proves volatile if not illogical.[16] But those who come to terms with Mann's kaleidoscopic view of the world will find it in "the power of the grotesque—the speed of psychological processes—the assured description of people—the perspicacity— the moral passion—the richness of maxims and aphorism . . ."[17] and many more of the author's qualities which are known from his earlier achievements. They will also be deeply touched by the modest pride with which a lonely and forgotten man looks at his own contribution to literature.

Like *Empfang bei der Welt, Der Atem* constitutes a life's summary, but with much greater coherence and sureness of purpose than the former. Also, in it the emphasis is shifted from a confused view of a cultural heritage received and a cultural heritage left behind to an analysis of two opposing *Weltanschauungen* and a commitment to one of them. Contrary to Ludwig Marcuse's opinion, *Der Atem* can be readily deciphered,[18] but it resists the quick glance and the desire for easy penetration. Only a real effort leads to its enjoyment, an effort like the one made by brother Thomas, who said,

. . . Needless to say that it represents something unique and incomparable in modern literature, or better: in the modern literatures above which it rises, so that one learns: above the languages is language. There emerges, with extreme exaggeration of a personal line, an old age avant-gardism which is known from certain cases (Parsifal, Goethe, and Falstaff), but which has here the effect of a brand new event. . . . . It is fantastic how the hard, why, even cutting, clear, and yet multileveled, cool, and overconcentrated essayism of the diction can be transfigured lyrically and what a moving effect is brought about by the element of excitement.[19]

A discussion of the work cannot help but justify to a large extent Thomas' enthusiastic reaction.

Against a background of political intrigue, the novel presents the last two days in the life of a strange woman. On September 1, 1939, when the Germans march into Poland, the financier Gabriel Laplace de Revers deems it necessary to do away with his bank president Conard in order to replace him with a synarchist. A struggle ensues between Laplace and his aide Comte X—also known as Lehideux—on the one hand, and Conard, Léon Jammes of the Deuxième Bureau, and a mysterious stranger, on the other. Both sides have helpers and sympathizers. Both sides concentrate their efforts on the moribund heroine, Lydia Kobalt, whose annihilation the synarch believes will solve his immediate problem, and through whose rescue the patriots intend to defeat Laplace.

Who are the synarchists? They are monopolists of power. Synarchism detests democracy and proposes "the common domination of all nations through their allied trusts which recognize no national boundaries." (19) In the text of the novel, the year 1922 is mentioned as the year in which the synarchic movement was founded. This explains both the origin and the meaning of its name, for 1922 is the year in which Georges Sorel died. Klaus Schröter, the first one to link Sorel and Mann's synarchism, says,

He [Sorel] had established the pseudo-revolutionary theorem of absolute violence and the name of "syndicalism" . . . . Any form of democratic parliamentarianism Sorel—following Proudhon—called indeed "anarchy." Heinrich Mann took this over in his blueprint of synarchism undilutedly; simultaneously, with polemic intent, he transformed Sorel's concept of "syndicalism"—in accordance with its true anarchic teachings—into the sound-related counter concept of synarchism, and further replaced Sorel's pro-proletarian irrationalism with the more dangerous aims of supranational trust politics. This was no arbitrary perversion of Sorel's doctrine: the works of this depressing eclectic gave sustenance to early Italian fascism, and influenced both Horthy fascism in Hungary and Franco fascism in Spain.[20]

Mann's synarchism reminds one also of a "society for the rationalization of Europe" which is founded by Schattich in *Die grosse Sache*, as Weisstein has pointed out.[21] One must, therefore, consider the possibility that Sorel's ideas already played a role in the author's thinking before he left Germany.

Schröter further recognizes existentialism as the philosophical basis for synarchism. He quotes from the novel, "A synarch is only concerned with being existentially without relation to the [unauthentic] 'one.' Existence does not belong to the world; inversely, it overpowers the world, fearlessly, and with disdain for life. A synarch boasts that we are born to die." And he comments, "There is no doubt that Heidegger's existentialism is reviewed here in excerpt, with fair accuracy, by the way, and under avoidance of its affected terminology.[22] Schröter's insight into Heidegger's achievement is perhaps subject to debate. Professor Weisstein may be correct in referring to the theoretician of existentialism in the novel as the "caricature of an existentialist." [23] But there is no doubt that Heinrich Mann agrees with Schröter, for the synarch theoretician quoted by this scholar is called Lehideux, the horrible one, and his name is brought into direct relationship with his philosophy.[24]

The woman whom the synarchists wish to destroy is known as Lydia Kobalt, but that is not her name. She is really the Baroness Kowalsky, née Marie-Thérèse Dolores Lydie Comtesse de Traun, de la maison Traun-Monteformoso. Her character owes something to Heinrich Mann's second wife. "Your memory of the woman makes it possible for you to understand the atmosphere of the novel, although she is represented with only a few of her words," Mann wrote to Klaus Pinkus. "The novel of my beloved it is, nevertheless. . . ." [25] But Lydia also owes something to Fontane's *Cécile*. Again Klaus Schröter must be quoted, who has worked out the parallels between Mann's last heroine and a character in one of Fontane's most underrated novels.

Fontane puts into the mouth of the Berlin court preacher Frommel [26] an anecdote: namely that Pope Gregory XVI, publicly importuned by a woman from the Campagna who "under continuous self-accusations" had asked for forgiveness, had turned from her "coldly and with defensive posture," saying " 'Una enthusiasta.' " This anecdote is echoed in Heinrich Mann's novel in slightly altered form: Lydia had broken protocol when as a sixteen-year-old she had been at the court of the last Austro-Hungarian King and Emperor and . . . had thrown herself at the feet of the monarch out of turn. The Emperor, *neither gracious nor ill-humored,* judged her: "romantic." [27]

Both Cécile and Lydia are guilty in the eyes of their skeptic authors. But Lydia's guilt, excessive emotionalism, is atoned for, like that of her spiritual ancestress Cécile, through her fundamental goodness.

Lydia's life is divided into three stages. As a young woman she has partaken of the mode of existence common to her social class, but with humor and without class-consciousness. After her husband's death in 1914, coincidental with the outbreak of the war, she falls upon bad days, refuses the help of her sister, the Princess de Vigne, works in a factory, becomes a Communist, and assumes the name Kobalt. And as the interim between the two great wars nears its end, she encapsules herself in an unreal world, walking daily to the Nice bank in her 1910 dress to ask for her millions, which never arrive.

Everyone knows her and her eccentricities, but those who knew her in her prime love her dearly, and those to whom she speaks are bewitched by her voice. No one realizes how sick she is. Her lungs are troubling her, and she often must "arrange her breath." Yet she keeps going, and during her last thirty-odd hours, the period encompassed by the novel, she regains her lucidity; relives her past; participates—an active victim—in the events precipitated by the outbreak of the war, and dies transfigured like a saint in the very moment when Laplace, her adversary, is shot.

The events are numerous. An unsuccessful plot to kidnap and kill her is followed by an equally abortive one to poison her. She receives money through Conard, who is infatuated with her. After a fainting spell she is lodged in the Hotel de Nice, where she used to stay when royalty filled its rooms and halls. Here she sleeps a while and has a meeting with Léon Jammes. Another brief nap follows. After this a Communist friend visits her and invites her to flee to Moscow with him. She does not do so, although the idea of leaving is always with her. The line from Baudelaire's "Moesta et Errabunda" ("Grieving and Wandering"), "Take me away, carriage! Carry me off, Frigate," is the counter-theme to her leitmotif, Ravel's "Pavane for a Dead Princess." When her friend leaves, she goes to the casino, gambles, and wins so much that she is rumored to have broken the bank. She attends a concert where the Pavane is played; she falls asleep once more; she rides with Léon Jammes and a mysterious character named Leslie Simmons Krapotnikow to a small café called "The Pig without Rancor"; again her Pavane is heard. And only after an evening of drinking, brawls, and clarifying conversation about the past can she return to the hotel, exhausted and ready to die, with numerous visitors attending to her needs and paying their last respects.

Crowded as the day is, one does not have the feeling of being rushed. The pace of the novel is lively, like that of *Die kleine Stadt,* but not breathless, like that of "Kobes." Precision rather than hurry distinguishes the style. This is a tour de force, since precision is used to describe imprecise memories and enigmatic aspects of life. Some of the figures gropingly search for their identity, their sense of self being shaken because others have so thoroughly changed over the years. Many are filled with ambivalent feelings concerning the heroine. Pithy formulations for the Protean in man's existence exercise a fascination upon the reader without parallel in Mann's other writings. And yet there is a straight line of thought, the kind of discernible attitude which one seeks in vain in *Empfang bei der Welt.*

Life as a game, to be lived and cherished, but not to be taken so seriously as to injure anyone; life as a good-humored joke; life as a sequence of errors redeemed by *Menschenfreundlichkeit*—friendliness of human beings toward human beings—this constitutes Mann's last view of things. Lydia has lived this kind of a life, achieving thereby a *Lebensgefühl* as intense as that of Violante von Assy. And just as in other Mann novels the general idea behind the entire work is gathered together and presented in the nutshell of a play, *Der Atem* presents its central point through a stage performance. Half awake and half dreaming, the heroine reminisces about the *commedia del arte* play of the Marchese del Grillo, which she saw with her husband long ago. Its story is the Christopher Sly story which opens *The Taming of the Shrew.* Used as an introduction by Shakespeare, but not fully developed; used in defense of a rigid class system by Holberg in *Jeppe on the Hill;* treated by Hauptmann neo-romantically in his *Schluck und Jau*—with a "double" motif and a social message thrown in—it becomes, in the hands of Heinrich Mann, the symbol of man's comedy of errors, of dreams full of yearning from which one awakens before the moment of fulfillment. Life is a disappointment, but the Marchese takes the sting out of this disappointment, his whims being tempered by considerateness. What is not to be taken seriously must not hurt either.

Empfang bei der Welt and *Der Atem* review their author's lifetime more thoroughly than does the autobiography. His era, so he maintains, consists of two phases, the period of exhaustion and the period of the holocaust. But in all periods the individual has ways of asserting himself and thereby giving his age a new quality. Identifying himself with his last heroine, Mann wrote in 1947, "Very well, then; the Austrian countess of the novel *Der Atem* lived in extreme poverty, but she died with distinction." [28] Mann knew that he would do the same, when, aware of his achievements, he wrote the last sentence of *Der Atem*: "The world slept as if paralyzed in the nights of its unleashed catastrophes, when we, too, are tired and put down the pen."

III *Summary*

Having surveyed the total body of Heinrich Mann's writings, one cannot help being impressed with its magnitude, its richness, and its importance. It possesses documentary significance because it represents an almost complete intellectual and political history of Germany in the first half of the twentieth century. But it also has real literary significance. On its level of excellence it is unique with regard to the interpenetration of artistry and moral *engagement*. Furthermore, through it the best thought of nineteenth century France entered German thinking. As a result, it contributed greatly to the escape of the German novel from its earlier provincialism. And finally, influenced as its author was by great minds, he in turn influenced poets and writers of undisputed stature.

Certainly Heinrich Mann's works do not strike one as modern in the sense in which Kafka is modern. For this Mann is too deeply rooted in the nineteenth century. Yet it is the modern world which he describes in all its Protean transformations. That he does so without Kafka's agony (or Thomas Mann's irony) makes him perhaps less interesting to the present generation than his internationally renowned confrères. In the long run, however, the strong inner tensions evident in his work may prove to be as intriguing and revelatory as Kafka's paradoxes and Thomas Mann's legerdemains concerning "truth." These tensions stem from Heinrich's "sentimentalic" character, to use Schiller's almost untranslatable term. They stem from an awareness of the discrepancy between life as it is and life as it could be and ought to be. As such they are independent from faith or the lack thereof. What has the effort to do with the belief in its success? And so, they go beyond the modern, being perennial and universal.

An overall appraisal should not obfuscate one's view regarding individual works. When it is a question of determining how well Heinrich Mann realized his intentions from page to page, it must be said that his legacy constitutes an ocean of words studded with beautiful islands. The islands, the works which have a fair chance to endure, are *Professor Unrat, Die kleine Stadt, Der Untertan,* the Henri Quatre novel, *Der Atem,* a score of novellas, and perhaps *Madame Legros.* In addition to this, it should be pointed out that some of Mann's characters possess qualities which exceed the literary. To be sure, they are no Hamlets, Fausts, or Don Juans. But Unrat, the petty bourgeois turned despot; Hessling, the loyal subject of an emperor whose histrionics are a poor camouflage for a hollow and valueless system; Kobes, the exploiter who understands neither the world nor himself; King Henri, and Lydia Kobalt, the aristocrats as democrats—these are splendid creations, well enough realized to leave their fictional contexts and to live as types in the minds of those who have read Heinrich Mann, be it for special reasons or purely for entertainment.

Notes and References

CHAPTER ONE

1. *Wir waren fünf* (Konstanz, 1949).

2. "Found unsuitable for the paternal business, a more than 100-year-old firm, a marine cargo company, grain import and export, the son would not have satisfied his father by becoming a dusty bookvender. . . ." Heinrich Mann, *Briefe an Karl Lemke and Klaus Pinkus* (Hamburg, n.d.), p. 86. Hereafter cited as *Briefe an Lemke*.

3. *Ibid.*, p. 178.

4. *Ibid.* p. 86.

5. *Ibid.*, pp. 44 f.

6. Heinrich Mann, "Kurze Selbstbiographie," Appendix to Herbert Ihering, *Heinrich Mann* (Berlin, 1951). cited hereafter as Ihering. This autobiographical sketch was sent to Alfred Kantorowicz in March, 1943.

7. Cf. Ulrich Weisstein, *Heinrich Mann* (Tübingen, 1962), pp. 261–264. Hereafter cited as Weisstein.

8. Weisstein, p. 7.

9. Thomas Mann, *Briefe 1889–1936* (Berlin, 1961), p. 130.

10. Printed in Alfred Kantorowicz, *Heinrich und Thomas Mann* (Berlin, 1956), p. 115.

11. "Kurze Selbstbiographie," Ihering, *op. cit.*

12. Weisstein, p. 9.

13. Cf. Golo Mann, "Ein Stück Erinnerung," *Du*, XX (December 1960), p. 74.

14. Werner Hegemann in *Das Tagebuch* (April 11, 1931), quoted by Weisstein, p. 11.

15. Heinrich Mann, *Ausgewählte Werke in Einzelausgaben* (Berlin: 1950 ff.), XII, 527. All thirteen volumes of this edition will be cited hereafter as *Werke*.

16. Reprinted in Thomas Mann, *Gesammelte Werke* (Berlin, 1960), XI, 476–480.

17. *Ibid.*, pp. 479 f.

Notes and References

CHAPTER TWO

1. *Briefe an Lemke,* p. 44.
2. Matthew Josephson, Preface to *In the Land of Cockaigne,* trans. Axton D. B. Clark (New York, 1929), p. 3.
3. *Werke,* I, 62. Numbers in parentheses after quotations refer to the pages of the appropriate volume in this edition.
4. Weisstein, p. 29.
5. *Die Göttinnen* (Berlin, 1957). Cited in the editor's notes, p. 757. In this section, numbers in parentheses refer to this edition.
6. *Ibid.,* p. 758.
7. Ihering, p. 23.
8. Roger A. Nicholls, "Heinrich Mann and Nietzsche," *Modern Language Quarterly,* XXI (1960), 168.
9. *Ibid.,* p. 169.
10. Both Kantorowicz and Weisstein stress the relationship of Don Saverio to several of the characters created by Frank Wedekind. Cf. Weisstein, p. 51.
11. Cf. *Die Göttinnen,* p. 765, and Weisstein, pp. 48 and 55.
12. Gottfried Benn, *Gesammelte Werke,* ed. Dieter Wellershoff (Wiesbaden, 1959), I, 415 ff.
13. Cited by Benn, *ibid.,* p. 623.
14. Weisstein, p. 48.
15. Kasimir Edschmid, *Lebendiger Expressionismus* (Munich, 1961), p. 306.

CHAPTER THREE

1. Weisstein, p. 57.
2. Alfred Kantorowicz, "Heinrich Manns *Jagd nach Liebe,*" *Die Zeit* (April 17, 1958), p. 5.
3. *Ibid.*
4. Quoted *Ibid.*
5. Heinrich Mann, *Die Jagd nach Liebe* (Berlin, 1957), p. 52.
6. Cited by Alfred Kantorowicz, *loc. cit.*
7. For the chronology, cf. *Briefe an Lemke,* p. 66.
8. *Ibid.,* p. 67.
9. J. Leslie Mitchell, *The Blue Angel* (London, 1932), p. 7. Unfortunately, Mr. Mitchell's appreciation of Mann's novel by far exceeds his ability as a translator; cf. Ulrich Weisstein's review in the *Yearbook of Comparative and General Literature,* IX (1960), 122–125.
10. The teachers, and especially the director, of Hanno Buddenbrook's school are mentioned by both Weisstein and Kantorowicz as

parallels, and even possible sources, of *Unrat*. See Weisstein, p. 66, and Kantorowicz in *Werke*, I, 633 f.

11. Cited by A. Kantorowicz in *Die Göttinnen*, p. 781.

12. *Das öffentliche Leben* (Berlin, 1932), p. 325.

13. Cf. Heinrich Mann, *Ein Zeitalter wird besichtigt* (Berlin, 1947), p. 176, hereafter cited as *Zeitalter*, and Weisstein, p. 66.

14. *Zeitalter*, p. 176.

15. *Ibid.*, p. 334.

16. For theories concerning the German novella, see E. K. Bennett, *A History of the German Novelle* (Cambridge, 1949), pp. 5–19.

17. Note Heyse's parallel comment on Goethe's *Elective Affinities*, referred to by Bennett, *op. cit.*, pp. 17 f.

18. Cf. Weisstein, pp. 67 f.

19. Hermann Sinsheimer, *Heinrich Manns Werk* (Munich, 1921), p. 29.

20. Ihering, p. 33.

21. Julia Mann's memoirs were written around 1903 and published under the title *Aus Dodos Kindheit* (Konstanz, 1958).

22. The word "race" as it is used in the title and the text has at this time no anthropological connotation for Heinrich Mann. It usually means nationality or, according to German usage, thoroughbred (as in *Rassemensch* or *Rasseweib*).

23. For a thorough discussion of irony see Erich Heller, *Thomas Mann, the Ironic German* (Cleveland, 1961), particularly chapter six.

24. Viktor Mann mistakenly calls Pardi "Leopardi." In the light of Pardi's character, Weisstein correctly calls this error a pardonable one. See Weisstein, p. 86 and Viktor Mann, *Wir Waren Fünf*, p. 119.

25. Thomas Mann calls this turn of events "ein bißchen populär verlogen,"—a white lie for the sake of popular appeal. Cf. Alfred Kantorowicz, *Heinrich und Thomas Mann* (Berlin, 1956), p. 87.

26. For the reference to Lord Acton, I am indebted to Ulrich Weisstein. Cf. Weisstein, pp. 87 f.

27. *Werke*, X, 667.

28. Félix Bertaux, *A Panorama of German Literature from 1871 to 1931*, trans. John J. Trounstine (New York, 1935), p. 135.

29. *German Life and Letters*, XIII (1960), 255–261.

30. Quoted by Kantorowicz in *Werke*, III, 414 f.

31. *Ibid.*, p. 416.

32. Heinrich Mann, *Das öffentliche Leben*, p. 339.

33. *Zeitalter*, pp. 276 f.

34. The town is modeled after Palestrina (Praeneste) in the Sabinian Mountains, where Thomas and Heinrich Mann spent some time

together. Thomas uses the same locale in the twenty-fourth chapter of *Doktor Faustus*.

35. For a discussion of the operatic plot and Heinrich Mann's corresponding short story, see Ulrich Weisstein "*Die Arme Tonietta,*" *MLQ,* XX (1959), 371–377.

36. Thomas called *Die kleine Stadt* "Heinrich's best" when handing the book to his younger brother Viktor. See Viktor Mann, *Wir waren fünf,* p. 292. And Heinrich stated in 1947 that his novel, conceived as a short story for *Simplizissimus,* "became in one and one-half years the most powerful thing I did." *Briefe an Lemke,* p. 46.

CHAPTER FOUR

1. Cf. Thomas Mann, "Über Königliche Hoheit," *Gesammelte Werke,* XI, 571.

2. Originally in *Pan,* I (1910), 137–143; most recently reprinted in *Geist und Tat* (Munich, 1963), pp. 7–13.

3. "Voltaire-Goethe," originally in *Freiheit und Arbeit,* 1910; also contained in *Geist und Tat.*

4. "As far as Germany is concerned, my first notes for the *Untertan* date from 1906." "Kurze Selbstbiographie," Ihering, *op. cit.*

5. The publisher Kurt Wolff had ten copies privately printed in 1916, for distribution among a few prominent persons.

6. *German Men of Letters* (London, 1963), II, 206 f.

7. *Briefe an Lemke,* pp. 90 f.

8. *Goethes Werke,* (Hamburg, 1962), VII, 616.

9. The link between masochism and sadism is also the theme of an excellent short story written in 1905 called "Abdankung."

10. Werner Mahrholz, for instance, reviewed the book quite negatively in 1919, but stated in 1930, "There are portions in his work— I am thinking, for instance, of the description of the *Lohengrin* performance in the *Untertan*—which are masterly as regards their wit, irony, spirit, satire and even power." Cf. Weisstein, p. 116, and Werner Mahrholz, *Deutsche Literatur der Gegenwart* (Berlin, 1930), p. 377.

11. Quoted by Heinrich Mann in *Macht und Mensch* (Munich, 1919), p. 48.

12. *Ibid.,* p. 94.

13. (Berlin, 1920). This work has not been translated into English. Numbers in parentheses after quotations refer to the pages of this edition.

14. Cf. Michel Vanhelleputte, "L'Essai de Heinrich Mann sur Emile Zola," *Revue des Langues Vivantes,* XXIX (1963), 510–520, and

Richard Exner, "Die Essayistik Heinrich Manns: Autor und Thematik," *Symposium*, XIII (1959), pp. 218 and 221.

15. *Macht und Mensch*, pp. 170–175.

16. *Op. cit.*, pp. 125 f.

17. With the exception of the worker Balrich, the main characters of *Die Armen* are the same as those of *Der Untertan*. Balrich, however, does not appear representative of his class in the sense in which Diederich Hessling emerges as typical for his. Only Balrich's change from a zealous hater of the rich into a zealous hater of the *Entente* may be taken as an accurate description of what happened to the German Socialist movement at the beginning of the First World War.

18. "A single play I took as seriously as my novels: *Madame Legros;* in February and April, 1917 it was performed in the Munich Kammerspiele and at the Lessing Theatre, (and went on from there). In front of the theatre I heard a woman say, 'Finally people can look into each other's eyes again.'" "Kurze Selbstbiographie," Ihering, *op. cit.*

19. *Zeitalter*, p. 226.

20. *Ibid.*, p. 225.

21. *Werke*, XI, 227.

22. Weisstein quotes from Shaw's work *Saint Joan* the sentence, "I will go back to the farm when I have taken Paris," and also points out the relationship of Mme. Legros to the figure of Judith. Weisstein, pp. 241 and 243.

23. Alfred Kerr, *Gesammelte Schriften* (Berlin, 1917), III, 110.

CHAPTER FIVE

1. Lion Feuchtwanger, "Heinrich Mann zum 75sten Geburtstag," *Centum Opuscula* (Rudolstadt, 1956), p. 562.

2. From an interview granted to *Les Nouvelles littéraires*, quoted by Weisstein, p. 142.

3. One might also mention Kafka, who had studied law and who made use of the Austrian bureaucracy, which he knew well, in both of his novels. In contrast to Musil and Broch, however, he was hardly concerned with the provenience of the conflicts and paradoxes in modern man.

4. The relationship of Heinrich Mann's essays to his total work and personality has been discussed at some length by Richard Exner in "Die Essayistik Heinrich Manns," *Symposium*, XII (Fall 1959), pp. 26–41, and *Symposium*, XIV (Spring 1960), pp. 216–237.

5. Félix Bertaux, *loc. cit.*

6. For detailed statistics on the inflation, see Richard Gaettens, *Inflationen* (Munich, 1955).

7. *Werke*, IX, 409.

8. Quoted by N. Serebrow from notes to *Der Kopf* kept in the Heinrich Mann Archives in East Berlin. "Heinrich Manns Antikriegsroman *Der Kopf*," *Weimarer Beiträge*, VIII (1962), 2.

9. *Ibid.*, p. 1.

10. *The Dial*, LXXIX (1925), 336.

11. Cf. Weisstein, p. 131, and Serebrow, *op. cit.*, p. 12.

12. For further echoes of Wedekind in this work, see Weisstein, p. 141.

13. Mangolf says: "I shall be one of the rulers and I shall look through things. I shall penetrate them and beyond that understand that such is life. The decisive day will be the one on which I shall be ripe for a second naïveté and act as if I knew nothing." p. 226.

14. Neither *Die Armen* nor *Der Kopf* is included in the thirteen volumes of the East German edition. According to Serebrow, *op. cit.*, p. 3, *Der Kopf* has been published twice in Russian, namely in 1937 and 1958.

15. Cf. *Briefe an Lemke*, p. 98.

16. Gerd Götz Rackow in "Sterny" is an example of the reactionary returnee, and Bibi, in the cabaret playlet of the same name, constitutes a kind of summary of Mann's opinion of the younger generation. In essence, the young people of the Roaring Twenties are excused because they have inherited a rotten world.

17. Weisstein, pp. 143 f.

18. *Werke*, V, 474.

19. *Op. cit.*, p. 136.

20. *Werke*, V, 20. Numbers in parentheses refer to pages in this volume.

21. Weisstein, p. 150.

22. *Der Hass* (Amsterdam, 1933), p. 126.

23. In the report about his brother addressed to *Freies Deutschland,* a monthly mazagine published in Mexico by refugee authors, Thomas Mann related the following: "To his niece Erica, my oldest daughter, he once said about us on a trip home 'Politically speaking I now have a fine understanding with your father. He is a little bit more radical than I.' That sounded extremely funny, but what he was referring to was our relationship to Germany, dear Germany, about which he was less angry than I for the simple reason that he understood things earlier and was not exposed to any disappointments. . . . He has had as much to endure from the German madness in torture and loss as I—even more so, since during his flight from France his life was in danger. But he is capable of not holding a grudge against the peo-

ple there, as I, for better or worse, continue to resent the loss of friends who graced my life. . . ." *Gesammelte Werke* (Frankfurt am Main, 1960), XI, p. 478.

24. Heinrich Mann, *Das öffentliche Leben* (Berlin, 1932), p. 330.

25. *Ibid.*, p. 333.

26. *Ibid.*, p. 335.

27. Heinrich Mann, *Die grosse Sache* (Berlin, 1930), p. 25. Numbers in parentheses refer to pages in this edition.

28. Ihering, p. 116.

29. *Werke*, XII, 175.

30. "Anmerkung zur *Grossen Sache*," *Gesammelte Werke*, XII, 740–746.

31. *Ibid.*, p. 746.

32. *Geist und Tat* (Berlin, 1931).

33. A 1963 paperback edition has a stylized drawing of Rodin's Balzac on its cover, as if thereby the gap were closed.

34. Quoted from the *Berliner Tageblatt* in *Die Literatur*, XXXIII (Oct., 1930–Sept., 1931), 697. On pp. 657 f. of the same journal, Weltmann has another review of the book which is full of praise, but which does not contain the idea expressed in the above review.

35. "Die Essayistik Heinrich Manns," *Symposium*, XIII (1959), 230.

36. *Ibid.*, p. 231.

37. *Ibid.*, p. 233.

38. *Ibid.*, p. 234.

39. Cf. *Werke*, XI, 471–497.

40. *Ibid.*, pp. 474 f.

41. Cf. A. Kantorowicz in *Werke*, V, 481–485.

42. "But conditions are not favorable."—Brecht. Since Heinrich Mann also wrote for the cabaret and was on good terms with cabaret performers, the quotation from Brecht is not intended to point to an indebtedness of the author of *Ein ernstes Leben* to the author of the *Three Penny Opera*. Yet it is noteworthy that the novel includes two cabaret type ballads in the tone of Brecht and Wedekind, whereas *Professor Unrat* contains only portions of a famous patriotic song. The beginning of one of the two is, to be sure, a cleaned-up version of a vulgar verse used also in *Professor Unrat*. Cf. *Werke*, I, 516, and V, 368.

43. Ihering, p. 117.

CHAPTER SIX

1. *Zeitalter*, p. 332.

2. In *Zeitalter*, Mann gives February 21st as the day of his departure (p. 336). But there exists a March 13th letter to his first wife

carrying the dateline Berlin. Cf. Stargardt, *Auktionskatalog,* No. 570, p. 55.

3. *Zeitalter,* pp. 376–385.

4. *Briefe an Lemke,* p. 136.

5. *Ibid.,* p. 98.

6. Georg Lukacs, *"Die Jugend des Königs Henri Quatre,"* Das Wort (1938), p. 125.

7. Cf. A. Kantorowicz in *Werke,* VII, 912, who cites the same parallels from the classics.

8. Weisstein (p. 163) and Lukacs in his review, pp. 129 f., object to Mann's analogies, the former for artistic reasons, the latter for political reasons. Kantorowicz (*Werke,* VII, 915) likes the use of history as a mirror of modern times, and W. E. Yuill (*op. cit.,* p. 216) merely notes the fact without comment.

9. *Zeitalter,* p. 392.

10. *Ibid.* The first sentence of *Zeitalter,* chapter fourteen, reads, "The France of King Henri Quatre and that of General de Gaulle are absolutely the same."

11. Henri, watching Peter Paul Rubens at work, says to Gabrielle D'Estrées, "Wie das arbeitet."—"How that works." This unusual impersonal construction, implying that a force beyond the control of the genius is working in him, has been attributed to Max Liebermann, whom Heinrich Mann knew and respected.

12. Weisstein, p. 163.

13. The unhistorical encounter of Montaigne and Michelangelo also fits into this context, for Montaigne's account of this meeting centers around Michelangelo's alleged descent from the Counts of Canossa. The philosopher reports that the great artist attributed his talent to his noble family background. (VI, 471).

14. Georg Lukacs, *The Historical Novel,* tr. Hannah and Stanley Mitchell (London, 1962), p. 320.

15. *Ibid.,* p. 321. See also Edgar Kirsch, "Heinrich Manns historischer Roman *Die Jugend und die Vollendung des Königs Henri Quatre,*" *Wissenschaftliche Zeitschrift der Martin Luther Universität Halle-Wittenberg,* V (1955/56), 1167.

16. Weisstein, p. 169.

17. In his *Deutsches Tagebuch,* I (Munich, 1959), A. Kantorowicz quotes Heinrich Mann as having taught him, "We know, that we do not live to see the victory. We can only dream toward it when finally we rest from the struggle."

18. W. E. Yuill selects a good example when he points out, "The plague that spreads across the Rhine is symbolic of moral infections. . . .", *op. cit.,* p. 217.

CHAPTER SEVEN

1. *Briefe an Lemke,* pp. 148 f.
2. The isolation was made almost complete by the death of Nelly Mann in 1944.
3. Ludwig Marcuse, *Mein 20. Jahrhundert* (Munich, 1960), p. 276.
4. "Der König von Preußen," *Die Neue Rundschau* (Spring 1949), pp. 186–192.
5. Masaryk had saved some of Mann's books and manuscripts when the writer had to leave Germany, and Mann had become a Czech citizen *in absentia* in 1936.
6. *Briefe an Lemke,* p. 99.
7. Thomas Mann, *Gesammelte Werke,* XI, 480.
8. Weisstein, p. 197.
9. Peter Blachstein, "Heinrich Mann besichtigt ein Zeitalter," *Hamburger Akademische Rundschau,* II (1947/48), 395.
10. Editors' post-script to *Ein Zeitalter wird besichtigt.*
11. *Zeitalter,* p. 190.
12. Thomas Mann, *Gesammelte Werke,* XI, 480.
13. *Heinrich Mann und sein Publikum* (Cologne, 1965), p. 86.
14. Letter to Fritz Landshoff, August 1, 1949, in *Deutsche Literatur im Exil* (Munich, 1964), p. 368. The critical portions of this letter may well have prevented the publication of *Empfang bei der Welt* during Mann's lifetime.
15. *Gesammelte Werke,* XI, 480.
16. Cf. Weisstein, p. 194. This scholar selects Mann's emphasis on youth and love as the author's "conclusion," and then points out that this does not follow logically from the sequence of action of the novel.
17. Kesten, *op. cit.,* p. 368.
18. Cf. L. Marcuse, *op. cit.,* p. 276.
19. Quoted by Heinrich Mann in *Briefe an Lemke,* pp. 112 f.
20. "Anmerkungen zu Heinrich Manns letztem Roman," *Grüsse—Hans Wolffheim zum sechzigsten Geburtstag* (Frankfurt am Main, 1965), pp. 136 f.
21. Weisstein, p. 192.
22. Schröter, *op. cit.,* p. 139.
23. Weisstein, *loc. cit.*
24. "In the first place he is Count X, really Lehideux. She merely needs to think of his philosophy together with his name, and she shudders." *Der Atem* (Amsterdam, 1949), p. 49.
25. *Briefe an Lemke,* p. 165.
26. Mr. Schröter erroneously calls the court preacher Frommel. In

Cécile he is actually called Dörffel, Frommel being the name of the court preacher in *Der Stechlin*.

27. Schröter, *op. cit.*, pp. 143 f.
28. *Brief an Lemke*, p. 58.

Selected Bibliography

PRIMARY SOURCES

Ausgewählte Werke in Einzelausgaben, vols. I-XII ed. Alfred Kantorowicz; vol. XIII ed. Heinz Kamnitzer. Berlin: Aufbau-Verlag,
1951 ff. This edition contains: I. *Im Schlaraffenland. Professor
Unrat.* II. *Zwischen den Rassen.* III. *Die kleine Stadt.* IV. *Der
Untertan.* V. *Eugenie oder die Bürgerzeit. Ein ernstes Leben.* VI
and VII. *Henri Quatre.* VIII and IX. Novellas. X. Dramas. XI-
XIII. Essays.

Die Armen. Leipzig: Kurt Wolff, 1917.

Der Kopf. Berlin, Wien & Leipzig: Paul Zsolnay, 1925.

Mutter Marie. Berlin, Wien & Leipzig: Paul Zsolnay, 1927.

Die grosse Sache. Berlin: Gustav Kiepenheuer, 1930.

Ein Zeitalter wird besichtigt. Stockholm: Neuer Verlag, 1945, also
Berlin: Aufbau-Verlag, 1947.

Der Atem. Amsterdam: Querido-Verlag, 1949.

Empfang bei der Welt. Berlin: Aufbau-Verlag, 1956.

Die Jagd nach Liebe. Berlin: Aufbau-Verlag, 1957. The notes to this
novel were published separately by Alfred Kantorowicz in *Die
Zeit,* April 17, 1958.

Die Göttinnen. Edited by Alfred Kantorowicz. Berlin: Aufbau-Verlag,
1957.

Die traurige Geschichte von Friedrich dem Grossen. Hamburg: Claassen Verlag, 1962. Contains the essay "Der König von Preussen."

Briefe an Karl Lemke und Klaus Pinkus. Hamburg: Claassen Verlag,
n.d. [1963].

Works by Heinrich Mann in English Translation.

Presently only *The Little Town* (*Die kleine Stadt*) is in print in
the United States. Frederick Ungar in New York offers both a
hard cover and a paperback edition of the original Winifred Ray
translation (London: Secker, 1930, and New York: Houghton
Mifflin Co., 1931). Therefore only the earliest editions are listed,
except for editions with different titles or retranslations.

The Patrioteer (Der Untertan). Translated by Ernest Boyd. New York: Harcourt, 1921. Also published as *Little Superman*. New York: Creative Age Press, 1945, and as *Man of Straw*. London: Hutchinson, 1947.

Madame Legros. Translated by Winifred Katzin, in *Eight European Plays*. New York: Brentano's, 1927.

Mother Mary (Mutter Marie). Translated by Whittaker Chambers. New York: Simon and Schuster, 1928.

Diana (First volume of *Die Göttinnen*). Translated by Erich Posselt and Emmet Glore. New York: Coward-McCann, 1929.

In the Land of Cockaigne (Im Schlaraffenland). Translated by Axton D. B. Clark. New York: Macauley, 1929. Also published as *Berlin, The Land of Cockaigne*. London: Gollancz, 1929.

The Little Town. See note above.

The Royal Woman (Eugenie oder die Bürgerzeit). Translated by Arthur Ashton. New York: Macauley, 1930.

The Blue Angel (Professor Unrat). Translator anon. [J. Leslie Mitchell?]. London: Readers' Library Publishing Co., 1931. Also published as *Small Town Tyrant*. New York: Creative Age Press, 1944. Retranslated by Wirt Williams as *The Blue Angel*. New York: The New American Library, 1959.

The Hill of Lies (Ein ernstes Leben). Translated by Edwin and Willa Muir. London: Jarrolds, 1934.

Young Henry of Navarre (Die Jugend des Königs Henri Quatre), trsl. Eric Sutton. New York: A. Knopf, 1937. Also as *King Wren: The Youth of Henri IV*. London: Secker and Warburg, 1937.

Henry, King of France (Die Vollendung des Königs Henri Quatre). Translated by Eric Sutton. New York: A. Knopf, 1939. Also published as *Henri Quatre, King of France*. London: Secker and Warburg, 1938–39.

The Living Thoughts of Nietzsche. Translation of Mann's introductory essay by Barrows Mussey. New York & Toronto: Longmans, Green and Co., 1939.

"Pippo Spano." Translated by Basil Creighton. *Tellers of Tales*, edited by Somerset Maugham. New York: Doubleday, Doran and Co., 1939.

"Three Minute Novel" ("Drei-Minuten-Roman.") Translated by Victor Lange. *Great German Short Novels and Stories*. New York: Random House, 1952.

"Abdication" ("Abdankung"). Translated by R. N. Linn. *Spectrum*, IV, No. 2 (Spring-Summer, 1960).

Selected Bibliography

SECONDARY SOURCES

The scholarly literature, except for dissertations, is not extensive. To readers of German the following titles are recommended:

EXNER, RICHARD. "Die Essayistik Heinrich Manns: (1) Autor und Thematik. (2) Triebkräfte und Sprache," *Symposium*, XIII (1959), 216–237; and XIV (1960), 26–41.

KANTOROWICZ, ALFRED. *Heinrich und Thomas Mann*. Berlin: Aufbau-Verlag, 1956.

SCHRÖTER, KLAUS. *Anfänge Heinrich Manns*. Stuttgart: J. B. Metzlersche Verlagsbuchhandlung, 1965.

WEISSTEIN, ULRICH. *Heinrich Mann*. Tübingen: Max Niemeyer Verlag, 1962. The most comprehensive study to date, containing the most complete H.M. bibliography.

WINTER, LORENZ. *Heinrich Mann und sein Publikum*. Köln und Opladen: Westdeutscher Verlag, 1965.

To those without a knowledge of German, the articles and essays listed below may be helpful. The titles are generally self-explanatory.

LINN, ROLF N. "Heinrich Mann's 'Die Branzilla,'" *Monatshefte*, L (1958), 75–85.

———. "Portrait of Two Despots: 'Auferstehung' and 'Der Tyrann,'" *Germanic Review*, XXX (1955), 125–134.

———. "Heinrich Mann and the German Inflation," *Modern Language Quarterly*, XXIII (1962), 75–83.

———. "Democracy in Heinrich Mann's *Die kleine Stadt*," *The German Quarterly*, XXXVII (1964), 131–145.

LUKACS, GEORG. *The Historical Novel*. Translated by H. and S. Mitchell. London: Merlin Press, 1962. Chapter IV entitled, "The Historical Novel of Democratic Humanism," deals extensively with Mann's *Henri Quatre* volumes.

NICHOLLS, ROGER. "Heinrich Mann and Nietzsche," *Modern Language Quarterly*, XXI (1960), 165–178.

WEISSTEIN, ULRICH. "Heinrich Mann in America: A Critical Survey," *Books Abroad*, XXXIII (1959), 281–284.

———. "'Die arme Tonietta,' Heinrich Mann's Triple Version of an Operatic Plot," *Modern Language Quarterly*, XX (1959), 371–377.

———. "Humanism and the Novel: An Introduction to Heinrich Mann's *Henri Quatre*," *Monatshefte*, LI (1959), 13–24.

———. "*Die kleine Stadt*: Art, Life and Politics in Heinrich Mann's Novel," *German Life and Letters*, XIII (1960), 255–261.

————. "Heinrich Mann, Montaigne and *Henri Quatre*," *Revue de Littérature Comparée*, XXXVI (1962), 71–83.

YUILL, W. E. "Heinrich Mann," *German Men of Letters*, Vol. II. London: Oswald Wolff, 1963, pp. 199–224. An informative introduction.

Index

Index